The Astrological Moon

Also by Darby Costello

Water and Fire
(The Astrological Elements Book 1)

Earth and Air
(The Astrological Elements Book 2)

The Mars Quartet: Four Seminars on
the Astrology of the Red Planet
(with Liz Greene, Lynn Bell and Melanie Reinhart)

The ASTROLOGICAL MOON

BY DARBY COSTELLO

Raven Dreams Press
Portland, OR

Published in 2017 by Raven Dreams Press
1434 NE Prescott St.
Portland, OR 97211
www.ravendreamspress.com

Previously published by CPA Press 1996
Second Printing 2003
Revised Edition by Raven Dreams Press 2017

ISBN 978-0-9840474-9-9
LCCN

Cover art: David Carillet
Printed in the United Kingdom, Australia and
the United States of America

TABLE OF CONTENTS

ACKNOWLEDGEMENTS

For those of you who attended these seminars in London: During the last two years, I have given seminars on the Moon in other places and other countries. Some of the material has been incorporated into the reworking of these seminars. Bridget Belgrave was invaluable, as a Mercury in Capricorn, Aquarian friend, in helping me to work streams of consciousness into sentences and paragraphs, via our shared love of e-mails zipping through the night.

Also, my heartfelt thanks to Teddy, to Jules – and to Stephen

2017 Update: I wish to thank Liz Greene, with all my heart, for giving me first the encouragement to write this book, and then the opportunity to have it published by the CPA Press in 1996.

And then, to Debra Kraatz, in 2017, for her willingness and enthusiasm in getting the work going for re-publication.

And to Tony Howard for his generosity in finally preparing the book for print with Raven Dreams Press in 2017.

PART I

The Moon as Source

Selene, Greek goddess of the Moon, Brygos painter, Vulci 490 BCE
Staatliche Museen zu Berlin

This seminar was given on 26 July, 1992 at Regents College, London, as part of the Summer Term of the seminar programme of the Centre for Psychological Astrology.

INTRODUCTION

Good morning. Today we are going to explore the imagery of the astrological Moon. I think it's fair to say that, of all the celestial bodies, it is the one that carries the deepest imaginative weight. By this I mean that more stories have been told about who it is, what it is, what it represents, what role it plays in our mythic and even literal lives, than any other astrological planet. It has been used in a very practical way by women for at least 30,000 years, to keep track of their menstrual cycles. It has therefore been connected with the feminine aspect of being, and most of the myths and legends that arise from the Moon are about woman. But that is not universally true – in some places it has been associated with the masculine and the dying-resurrected god images. But even this returns us to the feminine, as we shall see.

This is my plan for the day. I shall talk about the Moon in a general kind of way for a while, just to get our imaginations going. Then I will look at the astrological Moon as it expresses our earliest experiences of life. This is inevitably connected to the mother and her nurturing of us, first in the womb and then later in her arms – or in and out of her arms, to be more accurate. And then I shall lead us to think about our Moons as they express our capacity for intimacy with others and with life – for connecting to life in all its manifestations. The Moon reflects our connection with the source of life. By attending it we can develop a relationship with our souls.

Later I'll begin to speak about the progressed Moon. I'll see how far we get with that. I want to show you how, by attending it, you can experience certain dimensions of life, certain developments in your emotional life and your soul life. As astrologers, you can use its symbology to track the development of yourself from creature, to human, to soul – to one who recognises the place between time and eternity, and can draw nourishment from it, rather than being terrified and falsified by it.

For modern psychological astrologers, the Moon is connected to mothering. It says something about the kind of physical and emotional nurturing you experienced through your particular mother. The Moon also reflects the past in that it stands as a symbol in the chart for the container which collects all the day-to-day experiences of our lives. Everything that happens to us is gathered and held by the Moon. Its sign, position and aspects tell us the way that gathering takes place. And so it says something about memory. The Moon also describes the way we experience our connectedness to all life. It shows how we experience our common humanity in that we all require certain basic forms of nurturing for our survival; and we all have receivers for those basic needs. The Moon shows how we receive the basic kinds of nourishment we need for our survival. And since it is our mothers who first provide these – while we are in the womb and, later, in her (or a mother substitute's) arms – it describes our relationship to her.

So let us say that the moon in the natal chart reflects the kind of mothering (nurturing) one got, and further, the kind of mothering (nurturing) one expresses. And let us say that it describes the habit patterns and rhythms of daily life that are laid down right from the beginning – from womb-time – and reinforced over and over through the first few months and years of your life in your relationship with your mother. Now, what I would like to develop from there is how this mother experience, and the rhythms and habits of day-to-day life established very early, are the foundation for the development of your soul life. You can look to your natal Moon, and further to your progressed Moon, to keep track of the development of your soul life. This is what I wish to work towards today – the Moon as the starting place for the development of one's soul, and the progressed Moon as the navigational instrument, the symbol, for that place in us where we can track the soul's journey.

Audience: Darby, how are you using the word "soul?" What do you mean by it? Are you using it in the Christian sense of the word?

Darby: I am speaking of the soul as a metaphor for the dimension in ourselves between the non-material ideal realm – the realm of the God, or the gods, or the Eternal – and matter, the realm of the temporal, our matter, what matters to us in time-space. The soul, in this sense, is that which mediates between spirit and matter, between the invisible and the visible, between the intuited eternal reality and the manifest temporal reality. And this personal soul is our gateway to what has long been called the *Anima Mundi,* or the Soul of the World.

Words both touch reality and distort it, don't they? But I want us to look at the Moon today as beginning with a mother in time, but also leading us back to and forward to an eternal reality. This eternal reality may be also called mother – mother as life itself. Mother as the *matter* which mothers us as souls incarnated in time and space and which guards and treasures the spirit within us. The Moon in our charts describes the ways in which we experience receiving life's nourishment, first through our personal mothers. This relationship develops the habits and rhythms of daily life through which we seek and give nourishment to ourselves and others. We connect to others through this giving and taking, and through our connectedness we move on to connecting to life itself, and to Eternity through Time. All of this comes through the Moon, and through time seen in the developmental possibilities represented by the progressed Moon.

This morning we shall look at the natal Moon. We will remember much of what we know about the Moon from mythology and the discoveries of psychological astrology. We will speak about the Moon in various positions and houses and in its aspects to other planets. We will re-collect our information on the Moon.

For our very early ancestors, the Moon was probably more consciously significant than the Sun because it was the bigger light and it lit up the night in its cyclical way. The Sun was so much a part of day that you could say that it *was* the day. But the Moon had its rhythm, and all our night activities were determined by its waxing and waning light. Hunting for food certainly depended on the phase of the Moon. The quality of security we had at night depended on its phases. And as we awoke into consciousness, its connection with the female menstrual cycle became obvious.

But let's try for the moment to imagine what life would be like without the Moon. It would be so strange, such a different planet We would have day with the Sun – nothing would change there. And in different parts of the world there would be presumably different densities of Sun and heat and light, just as there is now. But night? What would night be like? There would be no light at all. Nothing but blackness.

Audience: Except for in the cities!

Darby: Yes, but would there be cities? Would life have developed the same way with no Moon? Let's imagine for a moment that life would have evolved differently if there was no reflected light – nothing to teach us about reflection, as the Moon would not have been there in the sky, reflecting the Sun's light for all those millennia before we had the elemental freedom to begin to reflect on things in our minds. Remember, as far as we know, the Earth was not the environmentally-friendly place it is today until about ten or twenty thousand years ago. The last ice age only ended in about 9,000 BCE. And – as far as we know – there was not much space for reflection until about 20,000 BCE, if we are to judge by artistic expression – cave paintings and bone, and horn carvings.

The stars would still have been there. We would have had this extraordinary background of stars against the black sky every night. The night would have been darkness filled with tiny points of light and the day would have been light. And there would have been nothing in between – no mediator. Dark to light, day after night after day after night, on and on and on. Year after year after year after year; light to dark to light to dark to light.

The starkness of it is very startling, because we are a planet that has a satellite that reflects the Sun, and night is the place of reflection, in a sense. Would we be an unreflective people without the Moon? Without the Moon, star light is not reflective light. Would we reflect on life? How much does our consciousness depend on the simple fact of the Moon, that mediator in the night sky that reflects the Sun with its waxing and waning, its dark and its full? Those of you who have lived away from cites for any period of time know the power of the presence of the Moon in its various phases, from a practical point of view, as well as an emotional or spiritual point of view – the Moon in relationship to the Sun, changing and waxing and waning all the time.

In early cultures, and in present day non-industrial places on the Earth, the power of the Moon is enormous. In places which are not electrified, the Moon holds sway over the night. Things happen at the dark of the Moon that never happen in the full Moon. Hidden acts take place when the Moon is dark, and the people do not go abroad once the Sun has gone down, unless they go for secret reasons. The full Moon is a time of celebration and night life. It is a time for emotional expression which cannot be expressed in the harsh daylight and is not felt or expressed during the dark phase. Emotions come out in full Moon which do not come out at any other time. Any of you who have lived in non-industrialized societies know this.

And even in our modern world we have traces of this knowledge. I once worked in a psychiatric hospital in New England. I was heading towards my degree in psychology at university at the time, and I worked there for my summer holiday between my third and fourth year. During the full Moon they put on more staff and they gave more tranquillizing drugs to the patients. We used to say they should give us the drugs too, to deal with the patients, during full Moon.

Audience: That last remark makes me want to ask if this was this in the 1960s by any chance?

Darby: Well, come to think of it…

Audience: It is also said that police forces expect more trouble at the full Moon and tend to put on more staff. But thinking about it, it is odd, because you'd think that criminals would be out more in the dark of the Moon, hiding their activity.

Darby: Yes, it is odd, isn't it? But I think the trouble that is expected has more to do with the loss of control over emotions that the full Moon brings out – the release of emotions, the freeing of inhibitions. We recognize that people who do not have much control over their own lives tend to become more frenzied at the full Moon.

Those of you who have powerful Moons, perhaps in water, and most of the Cancerians in the room, might recognize the power of the full Moon on your own emotions. You do not necessarily go out and smash things up when there is a full Moon, having enough nourishment, satisfaction, in your lives to channel your emotions. But you lunar people certainly recognise the power of the Moon as it moves and waxes and wanes.

The Moon has been connected with the nonrational side of life for a very long time, in our culture. And the nonrational has been considered bad, dangerous, to be avoided at all costs, for a very long time. We hear it in our word lunatic which the *OED* translates as "Insane; originally affected by an intermittent kind of insanity supposed to be brought about by the changes of the moon." And there was an added sentence I liked: "Formerly in Law, such mental unsoundness as interferes with civil rights or transactions." So, lunacy is the madness that interferes with Saturn's realm. Also, do you know there used to be someone called the "Master in Lunacy" who was "a legal officer with the duty of investigating the mental condition of people alleged to be insane." And then, of course, today we have the "lunatic fringe," in which category many people might put all of us in this room for talking about this at all.

There are stories of American Indian tribal women – is it Sioux? – who organise it so that they all menstruate at the full Moon. This is not as preposterous as it sounds, as any of you women will know who have lived in a dormitory or in a flat with other women. There are times when you are all in tune to such an extent that you are all menstruating together. You start out living together in your own physical rhythm, but over time you seem to adjust to each other until you are all in the same rhythm. And there is the story from Africa that certain tribes isolate their women during menstruation. They go stay in special huts down by the river during their periods. I don't know that this is true – I have not met tribes that did that – but I can imagine it is, and doesn't it sound like a wonderful idea?

Audience: Something both men and women would agree on for once!

Darby: Yes! Many of you know that, while living in South Africa, I worked at a museum called The Museum of Man and Science. The curator had a small, notched ivory stick which was said to be nearly 30,000 years old. It was called a calendar stick. The archae-ologist and anthropologist that had looked at it said it was a female menstruation calendar, because it had twenty-eight little notches on it. The twenty-eight notches were divided in sevens, and the four-teenth notch was especially deep. They said it must have been a lunar calendar for women. It makes sense to me. I held it and imagined a woman who carried it around with her and had a piece of grass tied to it so that she could move it up one notch a day. I imagined her part of a migratory tribe and I wondered if she had made it herself, or whether someone had made it for her.

But let's look at the etymology. My *Chambers Etymological Dictionary* (1947 edition) says that the Moon – which it describes as "the secondary planet or satellite which revolves round the earth" – is also another word for "month." It also says that it is the "measurer" and then, parenthetically, "of time." It says that the word for Moon come from the root *ma*, which means "to measure." This is so in all the teutonic languages; in Anglo-Saxon, in the Slavic languages, and also in Latin, Greek and Sanskrit. The Latin word is *mensis*. So: moon, measure, menstruation, month.

The stick reminds us that women and the Moon have been connected to each other as far back as we can reach in consciousness. The phases of the moon meant something to women, something very practical. This is one of the ways that metaphor begins, that symbols begin. Slowly, over ages, the Moon and woman's cycles become so intertwined in the imagination that they are part of each other. A bridge is built between them. These bridges, these metaphors, take us into the realm of myth.

CHAPTER 1

Lunar Myths

Moon as Queen of the Skies, Athanasius Kircher

There may be many other factors that lead us to the creation of myths, but the Moon in the sky, standing between our planet and vast space, and reflecting the Sun's light to us in its characteristic way, seems to be one of the most powerful. We have a propensity to seek understanding of patterns, to explain things to ourselves, to remind ourselves of things, to remember things. Women's menstrual cycles are connected to the Moon. When menstruation stops, the woman's body waxes until full, and she gives birth. Her body gets smaller again, menstruation begins again. She becomes pregnant again, and the whole process goes on and on – at least in pre-technological societies where birth control is not so certain. And then she is not the Moon, but separate from it and connecting to it again through menstruation. The Moon is associated with female and mother very early on.

GODDESSES

The Moon is associated with fe-male and with mother in most cul-tures that have left their traces on the Earth. There are moments in time where the male is associated with the Moon, but that is very rare, and very interesting. In these cases, the mother is the Sun, the eternal, and her dying resurrected son-consort is the Moon, dying, being born, coming to power, and then dying again. But for the most

Moon goddess and sleeping Endymion Roman mosaic Bardo National museum, Tunis

part, we know the Moon in her goddesses. We are familiar with our own Greek Selene and Artemis and Hecate, and Roman Diana. In India there is Shakti, who was associated with the Moon. In China there is Quan Yin, whom I don't know. In West Africa there is Yin Maya, and that is also, by the way, the name for "mermaid." So she is a mermaid and a Moon goddess at the same time. In Egypt there is the great goddess Isis.

In many cultures the waxing Moon, the full Moon and the wan-ing Moon have different names. The waxing Moon is the maiden, but she has different names in different cultures. The full Moon is the fertile woman, big with child. The waning Moon is the crone, witch or wise woman.

THE MOON AND THE DEAD

In *Symbols of Transformation*, Jung refers to the Moon as the gathering place of departed souls. Joseph Campbell associates the early cult of the dying resurrected bull-god of the Great Mother with the "horned moon" which dies, disappears, and then is born again three days later. He points us to the link between the Moon's constant, ever-changing story and our belief in one or another kind of resurrection after death.

There is a very strong early connection between the Moon and death. But it's not death in our linear sense – not death in the sense of leading to nothing. This is death as expressed by the Moon's relationship to the Sun – the cycle of new Moon, full Moon, waning Moon, and the death of the light in the dark of the Moon. It is death as the realm to which everything returns before new life can be born, death as the gateway to the new life. This is where the connection with the dying-resurrected gods comes in. In the *Vedas*, the souls of the dead return to the Moon to be devoured by maternal spirits. With the Trobriand islanders, the Moon is associated with female sorcerers who eat the dead.

Audience: Chinese?

Darby: Chinese I don't know. I only know the name, but not the story. Do you? In the Mayan cosmology, the Moon-Mother is called Maneater, which has gotten a rather pejorative meaning here. In the Orphic mysteries, which inform Pythagoras and his school, the Moon is the home of the dead, and it is a female gate through which souls pass on the way to the paradisiacal field of stars.

Audience: Can you say more about that?

Darby: Very little. Pythagoras is 6th century BCE, and was probably influenced by Egyptian cosmology. His teachings, his school, seems to have been surrounded by mystery or secrecy. He was both a philosopher, observing the natural world and its laws and a mystic, whose goal was bringing the individual soul into the Greater Soul. He is tantalising because we can't get our hands on his teaching directly. It seeps in through others. Scholars love digging down and trying to figure out what they were doing. The only thing we learned about Pythagoras at school was that he had something to do with the triangle, as far as I remember.

Audience: He didn't eat beans.

Audience: He probably played the triangle in an orchestra as well.

Darby: Do I sense the stirring of lunacy in the room? Well, he was working with the music of the spheres, the harmony of the universe as expressed in music and mathematics. And his teachings circled around a great deal of ritual. A lot of the ritual had to do with death and dying and the way to die to get back to the stars.

To get back to the stars, you have to go through the Moon. The Moon is our mediator to the Sun and the stars. It reflects the light of the Sun and it is our very own satellite. And it pulls our eyes and consciousness upwards with its ever-changing, ever-constant light. It draws us to look upward and contemplate the sky, and to notice the movement of the stars around us, and to begin to notice the changing and the unchanging world.

THE MOON AND THE BODY

Let me return for a moment to our bodies and the Moon. Various rumours from science tell us that the Moon's phases change the brain's electrical impulses. You can take the same circuit and measure it month after month, and the electrical impulses change in harmony with the Moon's phase. A friend sent me an article written by Laura Boomer last spring, in *Options*, I think. She cites huge studies done at various times, which show the effect of the Moon on women's cycles. There was one in Germany in the first half of this century which showed that more women ovulate, or menstruate, during either the new or the full Moon than at any other time in the month. She also notes that modern research done on women's menstrual cycles is very difficult because of the ubiquitous electric light. I was told recently that scientists who try to understand menstruation in women through doing controlled experiments have great difficulty. In trying to observe natural menstruation cycles through modern research, they come up against our modern world. Light affects hormones, and women who live in artificially lit societies develop rhythms that are not natural. Isn't that interesting?

Uranus rules electricity, and it was the first of the outer planets discovered. Women who have Uranus in aspect – especially in hard aspect – to their Moons have notoriously awkward times with their menstrual cycles in one way or another. Their natural lunar life, starting with relationship with ones mother, body, femaleness – is disturbed from the beginning. The natural rhythm between mother and infant is broken very early on, and the natural rhythms of the body and the emotions are disturbed. These aspects demand breakthroughs in consciousness. It is like being exiled from your native land. There is certainly a sense of loss, but inevitably an opening to new vistas of experience that take the tribe further.

Moon-Uranus women are cut off from natural lunar life and so are pushed to break through to another level of lunar experience. Moon aspects to the outer planets push us into exile and drive us to connection with new forms of consciousness – just as exiled people must find home in new lands with different tribes. The exiles are changed, and so are the countries in which they make their new homes.

But I wonder – do you think we are mutants? I sometimes wonder if, when they look back centuries from now, they will say our species mutated between 1746, the discovery of Uranus, and 1977, the discovery of Chiron.

Audience: Mutants can't breed, and we seem to be doing that all right.

Darby: True. Ah, well. Perhaps we are not so much mutants as an early version of the next step in our evolution as a species. Something is shifting in the body of mankind.

Audience: And today is the day.

THE HARMONIC CONVERSION

Darby: Ah, yes, today is the day of the Harmonic Conversion. It's certainly a day that is celebrating the potential of that shift.

Audience: What are you all talking about?

Darby: Someone told me that it marks a point in time when there was no longer any part of the planet which was not connected to another part through technology.

It marks a point where the leap is complete, and now we are completely connected – no more secret pockets of the earth to discover, no more tribes or birds or species to reveal. We are in touch with every inhabitant of our planet.

Audience: Is this good or bad?

Darby: I'm not sure these words apply. Though I think a lot of us feel fear and sadness at the changes that seem to be destroying the natural world. We cannot escape from the sadness, anger and fear over that. But there is a story going around these days, that we are actually evolving into something different, and that difference will change the way we are with each other and with the Earth. If we look at the technological advancements in the last few years, this can lead us to imagine that we are on the brink of a whole new way of inhabiting the Earth. And if we look at the destruction of the Earth over the last twenty years, we can also imagine that we *must* find a whole new way of inhabiting the earth.

The Harmonic Conversion is something about the intersection of our present consciousness with something new – a new shape. As far as I understand it, there is a new model that we are moving towards, and this is a day where we are touched by it. We are touched by the new archetype, with that possibility, with the new shape of consciousness to which we are evolving.

For most of us, this happens beneath our consciousness. But there are people all over the world who are gathering to be receptive to it. So I am wondering what, if anything, we will remember when we look back at this day. Here we are talking about the astrological Moon, but on a day during which lots of people around the world are meditating because they believe that something momentous is happening between time and eternity today. A new "idea" is incarnating. We are talking about the Moon, which is the symbol for our gateway into incarnation, and we are looking at it as the astrological symbol which may be used for the development from emotional experience to soul life. So perhaps we are part of it, whether we mean to be or not.

THE DISTURBANCE OF NATURAL RHYTHMS

Looking at people whose Moons are in hard aspects to Chiron, Uranus, Neptune and Pluto, we see people whose natural rhythms have been disturbed, and who are out of touch with instinctive life in many different ways. But we are also looking at people whose nature it is to struggle towards new forms of behavioural rhythms. These people have to shift into another gear in relation to their bodies and their souls. They have to find new forms for their relationship lives.

As we know, people with strong personal aspects to Uranus, Neptune and Pluto also often have capacity to transcend the ordinary, and to expand or deepen their awareness in such a way that it stands as a benchmark for new possibilities.

When the Moon is involved, this shift has to take place in the ordinary daily running of our lives. We cannot live in the ordinary way, and so we have to find new, wider, deeper ways for ourselves, so that we can reconnect to our bodies, our selves. We have to find rituals and routines that expand or deepen our connection with life, because the natural, instinctive life does not work, does not satisfy, is no longer natural. Aspects from Moon to outer planets may make it easier to be receptive to new evolutionary steps – if one hasn't gotten completely frozen by fear, and therefore shut off to anything except one's own personal events.

With outer planet activity to the Moon, there is a call to grow beyond one's own personal story. And of course, that is true with aspects to Saturn or Jupiter too – though one is not called out so far. People with strong outer planet interaction with their Moon are driven somehow to emotionally reach out beyond the bounds of family, tribe, town, home. The part of them that is foreign – foreign to natural tribal life – must reach out and touch people who are also foreign. It is easier for them to get on with those who are dispossessed than it is to get on with those whose rhythms are connected to nature; easier to be with other tribes than to be with their own. As these people reach out and connect with each other, new sorts of bonds are formed. New sorts of "families" are formed. It is all very new, as our technology which links us is still very new. But it is these unnatural lunar types who are the experimental grounds in which new possibilities take place, because they cannot find comfort in the old, natural rhythm.

THE MOON AND MIND

Audience: Is the Moon associated with the mind? I seem to remember that it is.

Darby: Mind is such a large word. If we use the word mind as the storehouse of memory, then the Moon is certainly associated with mind. Our Moon is the storehouse for everything that happens to us. Every impression from birth is carried in the dimension of us that is represented by the Moon. It is the Moon that records our experiences. Without our Moon, and what it represents, we would experience things and they would then disappear – no trace.

Audience: When parents ask, "Is my child intelligent?" do you look at the Moon or Mercury?

Darby: Parents do ask that, don't they, when you're looking at their children's charts for any reason. I am always surprised that they don't ask, "What kind of intelligence does my child have?" That would seem a more intelligent question. But to answer your question…

Audience: You look at both Moon and Mercury!

Darby: Yes. The Moon represents the natural mind or the natural intelligence, as distinct from Mercury, which is your capacity to gather information and bring to consciousness the information you need at any one time, and the capacity or incapacity to articulate it at the moment it is needed.

Audience: The Moon absorbs and Mercury articulates.

Darby: That's good.

Audience: The body is mostly water isn't it?

Darby: Recently I read Michel Odent's *Water and Sexuality,* his book on natural childbirth. He reminded me of the many scientists who have shown through their experiments that water "remembers,", retains traces of structures that are no longer in it. This is the basis of homeopathic medicines being prepared in water. He refers to human beings as "dynamic liquid crystals." Lovely, isn't it? Very lunar.

However, let's look at the etymology of our word "mind" before we conclude this particular thread. Mind comes from the Latin *mens* or the Greek *menos* and perhaps the Sanskrit *manas* – and they are all from the root *man,* meaning "to think." How about that? My *Chambers* says that "man" means, literally, "the thinking animal."

Let's take the word "man" in the sense of mankind for the moment, shall we? The species, rather than one half of the species. That way we can carry on here without controversy. I can see it rising in some of you. Etymology fuels political controversy. The word *mens* in Latin, according to my *Lewis & Short,* has the meaning of "the mind, disposition; the heart, soul – the conscience – the intellectual faculties, the mind, understanding, intellect, reason, judgment, discernment, consideration, reflection, etc." *Mens* seems also to be connected to the senses, in that to be out of one's mind is also translated as "out of one's senses." In Rome, there was a goddess Mens, who was the goddess of thought, and whose festival was the 8th of June. All you Geminis remember that!

Traditionally all those words that have to do with thinking, reasoning, discriminating are associated with *mens.* Now, perhaps we might associate all of this with Mercury. But as *Lewis and Short* says, *mens* is also connected to "the heart, the soul." And here we can put the Moon and mind together, although the word *mens* is not connected at root with the Moon. It is not a lunar word. But there is a kind of intelligence where the heart and soul are active.

The mind of the Moon as the heart is a place of knowing, and the soul is the container of all that ever happens to you. To learn, you have to be able to remember what you have absorbed. And although this kind of thinking does not come from a lunar word, its definition certainly draws us back to the Moon. So, what I am saying is that in looking at the learning capacity of an individual, you have to look at the Moon. Learning that does not include your Moon does not nourish you. It is through Mercury that you gather the information, but it is the ebb and flow of your Moon which absorbs it and assimilates it and makes it your own.

You take things in through your Mercury. But it doesn't become yours until it is part of you, through your Moon. When you repeat something that you have heard or read, then that is information. But when you synthesize the information and express it through your experience of it, that it is reflecting your lunar intelligence too. Our capacity to gather information is met by our ability to absorb it and make it our own. When you make it your own, the Moon has entered the field.

This leads me to remind us that, from an astrological point of view, to achieve your purpose, to let your Sun shine, to fulfil your destiny, you have to do it through the Moon – there is no other way. It is day-to-day activity, the daily rhythm of your own emotional and physical life, that provides the ground with which you achieve your destiny. We imagine our destiny through the Sun, but we experience our destiny, our being in life, through the Moon. The accumulation of experiences, some of which are remembered but much of which is carried beneath the surface, in the waters of our soul, is what gives form and rhythm to our existence in time. From a practical point of view, consciousness needs unconsciousness to be consciousness.

Audience: That's practical?

Darby: Yes! It's 9th-house practical – something about the nature of life. For example, a client who speaks the astrological language said to me recently, "I have Sun in the 10th house, but I have Moon in the 8th square Neptune, and this Neptune keeps me from dealing with the finances of my business in such a way that I can maintain success. It gets in the way of me achieving my Sun in the 10th. If only I didn't have that Neptune square to the Moon, I could get where I wanted to go." I said, "But it can't get in the way if it is taken into account. Dreaming or wandering or wasting time is at least half the equation of achieving your own destiny." To arrive at your own destiny, you can only get there by going day to day, through your daily activities, through the rhythms and habits of your daily life – through your Moon.

TRADITIONAL LUNAR RULERSHIPS

Now for some traditional astrology. The Moon has dominion over women, female, feminine (this is in all the old textbooks in my library – I like this). It is nocturnal, cold, moist, phlegmatic and fruitful. Really interesting images come out of those words. I address the men in the room. Think of your wives and women friends as nocturnal, cold, moist, phlegmatic and fruitful. Interesting, isn't it? These images have power to deepen perception. They are rich and dense, and slip past our socially adapted roles and ideas.

The Moon rules the breasts and stomach. In males it rules the left eye, and in females it rules the right eye. It rules "the public." We know this anyway through its association with Cancer. And it rules groceries, kitchen utensils, baking and laundry. It rules fresh water fish, sailing and brewing. Look at these things in your life and see how your Moon and its position and aspects describe your relationship to these things. What kind of a relationship do you have with your grocer, and what kind of a still do you have for brewing your brews? The kind of brews you brew might be your Sun, but your Moon is the still, and it also tells you what sort of still it is.

It rules bathing – is this sea, lake or bathtub, folks? Are you a bath or shower person? Do you spend long in the water or not? What are your rituals around washing and bathing? The Moon rules Monday; it rules silver. The people of the Moon are sensitive, emotional, domesticated, receptive, mediumistic, and are said to prefer living near water. So these are the people we might call lunar people.

Audience: You haven't stressed the Moon's association with the tides. I've been waiting for that all morning.

Darby: Well, I'm glad you finally mentioned it yourself! I often forget to mention the obvious, don't I? Of course – the tides, the sea. Seas have tides, and so do we. Our emotions ebb and flow, and when we are well with another person, the feelings between us ebb and flow. The tides show us that all water is connected to the Moon, and all water has its tides. Developing the capacity to accept those tides, recognising them, riding them, connects you to the waters of life and your own soul to the Soul of the World, the *Anima Mundi*.

Audience: Wouldn't you connect Neptune with what you are calling the Soul of the World?

Darby: Yes, I think I would, in all its mysterious dimensions. We probably have such a tiny understanding of Neptune's realm. But if you think of Moon-Neptune people, or those with Moon in Pisces, or sometimes planets in the 12th, they do tend to confuse – to "fuse together" – their own feelings and the feelings of others, and of the world itself.

MOTHER AND CHILD

Now, I want to look at our beginnings, growing from our own personal mother's bodies. And I want to introduce you to the work of physicist Danah Zohar. She has written a book called *The Quantum Self.* It got my mind sailing. It is a book based on the theories that come out of quantum mechanics. She has used these ideas to look at ourselves. Now, while she was writing this book, she was pregnant. She had been asked to do this book but she was pregnant, and they wanted her to do it anyway. So she was writing this book while the child was growing in her womb.

She expresses herself as a highly intelligent, in fact, an intellectual, woman. But she was pregnant while she was writing. So she spends long hours sitting there writing her book and feeling her pregnancy. She describes the process that was going on in her, and her pregnancy, and the subsequent birth of her child, while she was writing this book. She was educated as a physicist and a philosopher, but while she was writing this book she had some wonderful ideas, born out of her knowledge and her feelings.

I copied some of what she said about her relationship with the child within her, about the relationship of a mother to her child. One of the things she does is speak of the self as particle and as wave. She says, "The self is not just a thing. We are self as particle and self and wave." And reading that, I thought, "That could be a metaphor for the Sun and the Moon." One could say we are both particle and wave selves, and the Sun expresses the self as particle and the Moon expresses the self as wave. As Sun, my particle self shines from the centre of my being, shines on the earth, or in the air or through the waters, or simply shines as fire itself, depending on which element it is in. It may shine with a fierce light or a muted light, depending on its element and aspects, but it represents my shining light. But this self is also wave, and has a lunar side to it.

Since today we are looking at the Moon more than at the Sun, we shall be more interested in this self as wave. So let's look at this human need and capacity for union, again through something Danah Zohar says in her book: "The child is fused with the mother from the beginning and all through the first few months." She writes, "During the pregnancy with my first child and for some months after her birth I experienced what was for me a strange new way of being."

She is very conscious, and so is able to articulate this as most women who experience it would not. She continues, "In many ways I lost the sense of myself as an individual while at the same time gaining a sense of myself as part of some larger and ongoing process. At first, the boundaries of my body extended inward to embrace and become one with the new life growing in me. I felt completely self-contained, a microcosm within which all life was enfolded. Later the boundaries extended outward to include the baby's own infant form. My body and myself existed to be a source of life and nurture. My rhythms were those of another. My senses became one with hers and through her with those of others around me."

This is a woman speaking from the depths of her maternal nature – it is nature speaking, but through the medium of our modern language. Beautiful, isn't it?

Listen to this: "During all those months 'I' seemed a very vague thing; something on which I could not focus or get a grip, and yet I experienced myself as extending in all directions, backwards into before time, and forwards into all time, inwards towards all possibility, and outwards towards all existence."

You see why I like her so much? She is speaking from a deeply lunar experience. A child is growing in her body – and she is describing the feelings, the knowing that comes from that state. She is saying, and so beautifully, that through this experience she knows – actually experiences – the reality that we are also wave selves merged and merging with greater waves, which merge with even greater waves. We are connected to life through our own personal history and emotions, to human life, by sharing history and emotions with all other humans. And we are connected to life itself by being a direct descendant of all our ancestors right back to the very beginning of time, and even beyond, to the explosion of a star somewhere in vast eternity. And we share this with every living thing in the universe.

Sometimes one is self as particle and sometimes one is self as wave. Remember I am using particle and self, Sun and Moon, in a particular way. To light up the way, we might view our sense of particularity, and our sense of communality. Our sense of particularity we can associate with our Sun self – our sense of "communing-ling" our waveness. Self as particle and self as wave.

Audience: I think you might have made up a new word there.

Darby: That is the right and even the duty of Uranus in Gemini people. You see, it is as if she was moving through the days of her pregnancy, and as the Moon went around the zodiac she was touched by every possible manifestation of being, and it happened day by day, throughout all the nine months. She was connected to all life through this child growing in her body, backwards to the beginning of time.

And so, although your Moon represents your mother, through the Moon it represents *all* the Mothers and *all* the beings and *all* the creatures that we have ever been. You are born out of this body, who was born out of another body, who was born out of another body. So, although the Sun is the point in the chart which talks about the image that particularises you – your eternal image, spirit eternal, unchanging self – the Moon is how you access your eternity through the daily habit patterns and rhythms of your life. And in the beginning of this particular life, you received the form for those rhythms through your mother. But because all those other mothers are behind her, so to speak, we could say they collect into a particular archetypal mother, which is then reinforced and distorted and personalised by her.

CHAPTER 2

The Moon in the Signs

Athanasius Kircher The Moon as Queen of the Skies and aspects of all
the Ancient Female Deities, Obeliscus Pamphilius, 1650

The Moon is always in a sign, in a house, and in aspect. By understanding the sign through which your emotions express themselves, you understand which of the great twelve astrological images you feel most directly, through being born to *your* mother.

The sign tells you the astrological archetype through which you pick up, absorb, relate to, and respond to the rhythms of your mother. So let us say you have the Moon in earth. It is her *physical* rhythms and her *physical* nurturing of you that touches you most profoundly. She also talks to you, connects with other people, has her own passions and enthusiasm, has her own emotions. But what you most respond to is the way she touches you, and the rhythm. Because, remember the Moon is always about rhythm – the rhythm with which she picks you up and puts you down and attends to your physical needs.

As you are growing in her womb, you are absorbing all sorts of images, habits, patterns of communication and emotional history through her. But you are developing as a particular person. And this person emerges with his or her particular chart on the day of your birth at a particular time and place. The sign of the Moon says something about what you have been absorbing in that womb. And from the day of your birth, it focuses your emotional growth in a particular way. From the day of your birth, your mother's relationship to the material world will register most profoundly with you, if the Moon is in earth.

At the moment, I am thinking of two people, brother and sister, who were born out of a woman with her Sun-Moon conjunction in Aquarius.

Audience: You make them sound like race horses.

Darby: Well, one of them has Sagittarius rising and he is a bit like a race horse. The boy had Moon in Virgo and the girl Moon in Taurus. Neither of the children were like their mother when they were young, and she spent a lot of time trying to find herself in them, trying to get them to live her airy Moon way of being. But they responded to her physical rhythms and habits – they looked for stability and practicality from her – neither of which she could give in a completely natural way. Needless to say, both of their Moons were tensely aspected – the boy's by a square to Uranus and the girl's by a square to Saturn. Her children absorbed something that was not evident in her behaviour as a person – a practical emotional approach to life – but they absorbed it through her body. They reached down into their own ancestry, through her body, and found earthy lunar rhythms. Maybe they were evident in a grandmother or great-grandmother.

She never really understood her children, and they always wanted something from her she could not give. There was, fortunately, tolerance and love between them in the end, but they went through many disappointing trials. They were each asking her to be earth and she was relating to them through ideas. I think the love sprang from the way she probably tended them as infants, when she was caring for their physical needs as infants. Somehow that was remembered in their bodies. But by the time they were in their early teens and needing her to be simply there for them, she was trying to inform their minds in a particular way, and they didn't want that from her. Later in their adult years, they both had to find ways to let go of their expectations and find their own inner resources and their own modes of emotional sustenance.

Audience: My mother has Moon in Capricorn, and both my brother and my sister have Moon in water – Cancer and Pisces. They really seem to need something from her that I simply don't.

Darby: Where is your Moon?

Audience: It's in Virgo – I suppose that is obvious.

Darby: Well, it does tell us why you might not need the same thing from your mother as your siblings. The Moon seems to pick up a particular thing in your mother, and through that element you remember your mother. In water, no matter how well she nurtures you physically, and no matter how much she speaks to you and communicates with you, and no matter how much she loves you with her energy, her passion, her enthusiasm, what you register are her inner emotions. You are attached to her in the deep waters of your being, and your capacity to feel nourished and abandoned is greater than with any other element. Unless your mother has lots of water elsewhere, those two watery Moons are seeking moisture in a dry landscape – and probably finding it too, and giving it back. Your child's Moon will tell you what that child has to give you – what element will be given to you as you nurture it.

You are born with the Moon in a particular place. One month later, the Moon, moving on from this moment when you were born, has touched every planet in the chart. That is the first whisper of your emotional life set down. Two months later, the Moon has gone around again and touched every aspect in the chart and returned to its own place. Three months later, it has done it again. By the first year, it has done it thirteen times. By the second year, it has done it twenty-six times.

In the very beginning you can almost sense or see the kind of things that this particular child will respond to emotionally. What you do consciously or unconsciously has very little to do with it. The Moon is the part that will be set off, no matter what you think. You know how most mothers think, "My child will be different, I'm going to do it right." And most mothers give their whole selves to this task. But the child absorbs what it will from the mother's body and soul. We might say that when the Moon is in fire, it will absorb the mother's energy and imagination. It is attuned to her inner images – the images that drive her forward. Whereas the Moon in air absorbs from her the ideas and patterns of mental communication that are part of her ancestry, the patterns of information-gathering and expressing. If you have the Moon in air, then the urge to articulate ideas with words is deeply connected with your emotional connection to her.

Audience: I have Moon in Gemini, and I recently discovered that if I am misunderstood – even when discussing something quite remote

– I get very upset indeed. I know it's a cliché, but I really do feel that my mother never understood me. She has Moon in Scorpio, and I think she often feels abandoned by me.

Audience: I have Moon in Scorpio, and my mother has Moon in Gemini. I'm always trying to get her to keep quiet. And I can see she finds me a complete mystery.

Audience: Will you say something about each of the signs?

Darby: Yes. I was planning to do that sometime today, and now seems as good a time as any. I won't have time to go into detail here, but I'll give indicators in terms of what I am saying about the Moon in general. One day, I shall pull all my notes together and write it up fully. I promised Howard I would do that, and one day I shall sit down and really do it.

THE MOON IN THE FIRE SIGNS

But for now, just now I said that when your Moon is in fire you absorb through your mother's energy and imagination. It is through her, and reflected in her behaviour, but it is deeper, in that it comes through her from the fiery women in your ancestral life. It is really your take on her, whether she feels that way about herself in general or not. This energetic, imaginative emotional nature is your soul's way of engaging with life. You absorb it from her, and make it your own, over a lifetime.

So, when you are born with Moon in Aries, you pick up the heroic, selfish, aggressive, thoughtless, heedless, and self-sacrificing.

Audience: Aries? Self-sacrificing?

Darby: Yes, haven't you noticed that? As selfish as they can appear, there is a huge streak of self-sacrifice in their makeup. I think it comes from the heroic impulse which informs Aries, the longing to throw oneself in front of the canon to rescue the village, to be hailed – alive or dead – as a hero. The need to win honour through courage is enormous. And when it comes through the Moon, it expresses itself in the ebb and flow of emotional courage and fearfulness. One relates to one's mother as if she is selfish, and her most selfish traits are reflected in the child, but also her most courageous ones.

In Leo, the Moon has a rather grand conception of itself and life. Mother was a queen, and whether she was the wicked queen or the good queen depends on other things. For many of us with Pluto in Leo, she was often the bad or mad queen. But not always, of course; she may have been simply powerful, in a Plutonian way. For those of you with Neptune in Scorpio, she was possibly the sad or lost queen. But she was your queen and she better live up to it, or you do not forgive her. You absorb a sense that the day-to-day activities of your life absolutely must afford you pleasure or, at least, power – and a sense of outrage when they don't.

And in Sagittarius, you absorbed through her body and soul every adventurous, philosophical or dreaming ancestor in your line. You felt her restlessness very much, and any longing she had for a future, free of the daily grind.

THE MOON IN EARTH SIGNS

Those of you with earth Moons were attuned to her capacity for practical dealing with life. Aspects will tell you whether she fulfilled your need for this, as I said before.

In Taurus, you absorbed her need and capacity for material security, and her attunement to natural beauty. Through her, you received a capacity to care for your bodily needs and the natural emotional need for physical security.

In Virgo, you received her attention to health and the rituals of an ordered daily life. All the careful craftsmen and craftswomen, all those ancestors particularly sensitive to physical environment, resonated through your emotional body. For those of you with Neptune in Virgo, and especially when conjunct your Moon, this attention was amplified and at times almost deified. I have a friend who lost her way for a while and she told me that resuscitating her rose garden brought her "back home to God's world" as she put it.

In Capricorn, you picked up the chord in your ancestry that was sensitive to social position through social interactions. You were born with an incipient awareness of the mores of your society. You responded deeply to her social awareness and her need to be considered a valuable or respected member of her community.

THE MOON IN AIR SIGNS

Being born with an air Moon led you to absorb the intellectual ideals of your ancestry – an awareness of the power of communication. What your mother thought about, and how she used words and ideas – you were sensitive to these aspects of her nature.

In Gemini, you were most sensitive to her way of using words, her communication skills. You were attuned to her conversational method, and to all the wordsmiths in your ancestral line. If you have Uranus in Gemini as well, words are probably the way to wisdom, or enlightenment.

In Libra, you absorbed, through her, the chord that runs through your past that had to do with communication of ideas concerned with ideal behaviour. You registered her gifts and weaknesses in communication in such a way that "bad communication" was painful to you and "good communication" was restful. Those with Neptune in Libra felt this more keenly. An emotional need for grace and harmony was attached to your generation's need for peace and harmony. Emotional atmospheres that were too intense made you feel lost, confused or guilty.

In Aquarius, you took on the traits of all your most idealistic ancestors. Your mother's ability to be at ease with different kinds of people was emotionally painful or satisfying to you. Her own personal ideals mattered to you. Her eccentricities were interesting to you and you felt fine with them, as long as they were not elitist. You absorbed her social judgments and, depending on aspects, you approved or disapproved.

THE MOON IN THE WATER SIGNS

And when your Moon is in water, you absorbed from her the basic creature instincts. You picked up, through her emotional rhythms, the basic human instincts for self-protection and the protection of others. You were woven from the waters of your ancestry, with all the most fundamental human creature needs.

With Moon in Cancer, you felt through her the deepest maternal rhythms and needed, perhaps even more than those with other Moon positions, a regular pace in your nurturing – feeding, warmth, physical closeness in a rhythmic way. Those of you with Uranus in Cancer, and especially close to your Moon, might have had that rhythm interfered with by modern psychological attitudes on mothering.

Audience: Dr. Spock!

Darby: Ah, yes. Anyway, something interfered, but then with most of us, something interferes with our infant needs – but more of that later. Pluto in Cancer people, with Moon in Cancer, had the war, didn't they?

And so, with Moon in the heavy waters of Scorpio, the basic instinct for self-preservation operates through an acute sense of danger and a strong instinct for fight or flight in close emotional situations. This Moon was born to a mother whose situation intensified the emotional heritage of ancestors who lived in terms of risk and danger. The inherited traits of emotional privacy and fierce defence of emotional rights are constellated in Moon in Scorpio.

The urge for self-protection with Moon in Pisces is most paradoxical, as one would expect. This Moon picks up the ancestral chord that connects to all sorts of people in the past. If it singles out any, they are probably deeply religious or deeply lost. The self-preservation urge is merged with the sense of being everyone, and so compassion is often the response – "If I am you and you hurt, then to care for myself, I care for you." But it is often more subtle and often more confused than that. I see I could go on and on here, and I want to stop for a bit. Let's have tea!

FATE AND FREEDOM

Is everyone renewed now? Amazing how nourishing a cup of tea can be at the right moment. Let's go on to some of the questions that I could feel emerging in the room.

Audience: You are speaking about the sign of the Moon as if it is something that is predetermined – as if it is already decided by the time of birth. Do you think that is the case? And the house and aspects as well?

Darby: Hmm. Yes, I do think the sign is, well, let's say it is determined over the time in the womb. I don't know if it is determined from the moment of conception, but it seems to be something that grows into something "solid" over the months. A mother will know her child quite deeply by the time it is born, and yet there is something also absolutely unknown.

From what I have seen, the recognised bit can be described by the sign of the Moon, and the unrecognised bit seems to be described more by the Moon's house, and in some ways possibly the aspects – although it is not uncommon for a Moon-Mars woman to have an Aries-Moon child. But I have come to believe that the sign is the deepest layer in the sense that it reflects the ancestral memory of the child and traits that were three generations ago appear through the Moon sign.

Audience: I have Moon in Aries and I certainly don't feel energetic and courageous – mostly I feel like an angry wimp.

Darby: You are one of the Neptune in Libra generation, aren't you? Are they in opposition?

Audience: Yes and I put all the blame on that.

Darby: Oh, dear, you mustn't push my "blame the planets' button." I can go on for hours. I'll just limit myself to saying that your Moon in Aries is as gutsy and selfish and heroic as any other Aries Moon, but you incarnated into a time where grace and harmony and peace were idealised. And so the urge to fight was sabotaged early on by the collective ideal. Mother probably played out the confusion by masking her selfish instincts, her courageous instincts with this ideal. You incarnated with all the Aries instincts picked up from your ancestral line, through her, but you incarnated in a time where this was not collectively honoured. And it is important to seek understanding of why this might be and what might be your soul's journey, taking into account these conditions rather than blaming them. The opposition between instinct to impulsive action and a collective spiritual ideal that reads "God/Perfection is harmony and peace" sounds like an interesting field in which to grow a soul.

Audience: Why does Aries always get in first?

Darby: Silly question.

Audience: Yes, I knew it was. But my Moon in Gemini allows that. You didn't say very much about Gemini – I thought you would have had lots of words about that Moon.

Darby: You did? I wonder why that might be? Ok for those of you who don't know, I have Moon in Gemini too. Now what did I say? Well let me just say this: Moon in Gemini people are quite highly strung – usually sensitive to noise and dependent on words to give them something of value. I have a friend with Moon in Gemini who once told me that books had been her mother. Her mother had not been very kind or caring of her, and she learned to read at a young age and had an abiding love for books because she had, as she said, learned everything about life from books. She was pretty smart, so I guess she had read the right books. She went from listening to her mother, rejecting her quite early, then to reading books obsessively, and finally to teaching. She's a truly great teacher too.

Audience: I like good books, but I read a lot of rubbish too. I like good conversations, but I chatter too much sometimes. Or I think other people do!

Darby: The double-souled Moon in Gemini. I sympathise! So, before we go on to other things, let me give you another Danah Zohar quote. "To a very large extent, the baby's experience is the mother's experience and he begins to weave himself using his mother's cloth." And, "He takes in his mother's responses to the wider world for protection, for emotion, for care, and lays them down in his own quantum memory system. They become the stuff of which he is made and influence the development of neural pathways in his own brain." I would only add that her experience is not just what is happening to her in present time, during the pregnancy, but it is also all the things that have happened deep in the inner layers of her psyche, in her cells, passed down from mother to mother from the deep past. And what we have been talking about is how this manifests itself through the sign in which the Moon inhabits at birth. The sign tells us which of the twelve major chords that make up this musical scale called humanity has been struck, and so will be an underlying, constantly recurring note throughout the life, in all the ways that life brings.

You were grown in the womb of a woman with a history which is written in every cell of her body. You incarnate through that gateway, that woman, that history, and part of the package of incarnating into this world is taking on that history, through the rhythms that are her body. Those rhythms, those habit patterns of response, are partly a result of things that have happened to her in her lifetime, choices she has made, circumstances she has created, or have been created out of her responses. But they are only partly due to her life's experience. More deeply, they are the rhythms that she inherited from her parents and their history, from her mother's womb, which were inherited through the womb before that, and downward into forever. You receive all of that through growing in her body, and once you are born, the second stage begins, with her nurturing of you.

Audience: At the moment it is sounding all very fated and inescapable.

Darby: Patterns are repeated over and over, passed down from womb to womb, but each time is brand new. Each one of us inherits a depth and weight of history through the particular mother, or gateway, we are born through. Yet – and this is important, and gives us our terrible sense of responsibility as creatures – each of us is new and unique, because of the combination of mother and father, seed and egg. Each of us has a history, and each of us is brand new, never before a combination like this particular one. The planets go round, and every moment is the same, but has never been before, as each planetary combination has never been before. Cycles are ever-repeating and the total combination is always new. Like us – always the same and always at the very edge of the unknown, fated and completely free. Interesting combination, isn't it. No wonder we get so confused.

Do you have a question?

Audience: No, I just look like this when I'm interested and con-centrating.

Darby: Ah ha. You also look worried.

Audience: I have Moon in the 3rd conjunct Mercury, in Virgo.

Darby: Perfect! If you stop looking worried, I'll start getting wor-ried. So, what I am saying is that we each pick up a particular strain, a chord, a theme to which we will always return, and that is revealed by the sign in which the Moon is placed.

CHAPTER 3

The Moon in the Houses

Now I would like to go on to the houses – just a brief take on each house to give you the key ideas, to remind you and to awaken you to the possibilities contained by each house. I want to give you a framework from which to observe rather than the detailed conclusions of my years of observation.

Selene, Moon Goddess Meidias Painter 450–400 BCE Kunsthistorisches Museum, Vienna

Audience: We'll get that in your book presumably.

Darby: Oh I do hope so! So, onwards. The house in which the Moon is placed says something about the area of life in which your creatureness is most evident, where your creature needs are most highlighted, where the ebb and flow of daily life register most consistently.

Before you are born, the days go by for your mother, and a sense of expectancy builds up. Closer and closer the time comes, and now the hours are ticking round. Somewhere in your mother's body there is a deep expectancy, although if she is a modern woman she may be out of touch with this, and so lets other people decide when her child will arrive. But even when all the adults have decided when the child will arrive, it can surprise. Events are not as much in our control as we would often like to believe. Who knows how we individual particles are moved around by greater patterns than we can perceive? All we know is that there comes a moment when labour begins and there is a moment when the child arrives. You might say the roulette wheel stops there. And in doing so, the planets are set in their houses. One day an astrologer draws up a chart of that moment of birth.

We consider the configuration of planets and stars and we draw out the Moon and its conditions to understand the child's early emotional environment. This environment is the mother. We note the sign to catch the archetypal mother this child will seek to draw out of this human mother, and we note the house. The house tells us where this child will feel the ebb and flow of physical and emotional nourishment from the mother – which area of life will be activated every month, most strongly during the first months and years of life, by events with the mother. These will be reflected by the transiting Moon and by the planets touching that position. And later, the house tells you what part of life's process you will feel most at home with. Whether "home" is a comfortable feeling or not depends on other things. The Moon's house tells you where the emotional habit patterns of daily life will nourish you, where you will feel the ebb and flow of life's ever-changing, ever-the-same abundance

One more thing. The house position tells us what our mother was paying attention to when she wasn't paying attention to us – or, to put it more finely, what area of life she was attending and we were registering most consistently during our first few months and years of life. This is where the ebb and flow come in – she was with you; she was not; with you; not. Where was she when she was not? I mean where was she in her attention? A 10th house Moon, her social position or area of mastery; a 6th house Moon, her work, or health; a 9th house Moon, her dreams, plans for the future, people in other places. The ebb and flow of her caring for you is felt to be connected to these things. Later, these things become the source of your emotional ebbing and flowing in that you were full and emptied out here. Your emotional gifts and needs are expressed here. And you connect to the deepest sources of life through these areas. Your soul develops – your connection to life's rhythms express themselves here.

Let's look at the houses in sequence, as house systems and cusps vary, and also because the houses have a sequential beauty that orders our thought – well, my thought anyway!

Audience: What about the differences in house systems which can put your Moon in different houses.

Darby: Yes, that is a problem.

Audience: And?

Darby: And I'm not going to address it here. You have to find the house system that speaks to you most clearly. For now, I don't want to get distracted into that.

When the Moon is in the **1st house,** the infant will register most powerfully the mother's need to survive – the mother's need to stand up for herself and be seen, perhaps by her husband, but certainly by someone significant. The infant will grow to recognize its mother's rhythms of security and anxiety on this account Like any infant geared for survival, it will "use" this information in that it will attune itself to her need for survival. People with their Moon in the 1st house usually see their mothers as "survivors." Later, any crises in emotional relationships feel like survival issues. "I can't survive without you – I can't survive with you hanging on to me." And going out and doing things for survival will connect you to life's source.

The Moon in the **2nd house** registers and reinforces in the mother any tendency to equate security with ownership. Her attention to the natural world and her attention to the things she herself owns is registered in the ebb and flow of her nourishment of the child. You know it's an odd thing, perhaps, but I have never met anyone that I can remember with a 2nd house Moon that does not value and love his or her mother. I am sure there are people who would challenge this perception – but it seems a powerful position for closeness. Perhaps it's a deep sharing of values? Perhaps a mother who opens you to the beauty of the natural world as she nurtures you can be forgiven a lot. Development of your natural resources connects you to the rhythms that nourish you.

Those with the Moon in the **3rd house** record their mother's attention to other things in her environment – things such as the comings and goings of other people around her, and the day-to-day news that filters through. This child's sibling position is important and the rhythms of nourishment are connected to things which may seem to distract from that nourishment. Reading and talking to others nourish, and this is also where you will feel most undernourished when these things are neglected.

Audience: What do you mean by that?

Darby: I mean that I have noticed that people with 3rd house Moons are often frustrated by what they call "distractions" from what they are most emotionally engaged with. And when I have been with mothers of 3rd-house-Moon children, I notice these children's frustration with their mother's distractions from them. I think they are particularly attuned to these distractions and later their emotional development will depend on their ability to accept, include, tolerate, and deal with the distractions of day-to-day life – and yes, distractions in conversations, of course. I have a dear friend with Moon in Aries in the 3rd, and we are part of a study group translating early astrological manuscripts. Whenever we get too far away from the text, she starts getting edgy, and suddenly burst out with, "Can we get back to the work?" For some reason this delights me.

Infants born with Moon in the **4th house** register their mother's family connectedness very powerfully. She is felt to be someone who is part of a family, and so survival for the infant develops as survival within the family. As the Moon goes around in the sky every month and makes various aspects to the natal Moon, it reinforces this connection between the sign of the Moon and the family life. Each time it goes into the sign of the Moon, the child absorbs the family dynamics with its emotional and physical nurturing. And there is a deep awareness of grandmothers with this position, but I have not noticed that there is more awareness of father's mother than of mother's mother. When cut off from your family, you have to seek connection with the deeper family – the roots of family life, the rhythms of nature as family itself.

Audience: Does it indicate a very close relationship with the mother? I have Moon in the 4th and I don't like my mother at all!

Darby: I have a close friend in her late sixties who has Moon in Libra in the 4th. She was adopted and was indifferent to her natural mother and disliked her adopted mother. But she was fascinated by her own emotional history and even wrote a book about it. I think it is a deep emotional tie to your background and whether the tie is comfortable or not depends on other things. It is simply that the ebb and flow of emotional and physical care are strongly connected with your mother's family feelings and you register this in her and reinforce it in her throughout your infancy and even in your adult interactions with her.

The Moon in the **5th house** is attuned to the mother's capacity for self-expression and delight. Each time the transiting Moon touches this natal Moon, this infant records its mother's creative, vital interaction with her child and with life itself. I think that this position feels centre-stage in its mother's life – and whether the centre of the stage is a happy or unhappy place depends on other things. The infant registers the dramatic possibilities between itself and its mother.

A **6th house** Moon registers, day after day and month after month, the rituals and routines that attend its nurturing. It is attuned to the tidying-up processes and absorbs the mother's attitudes to such rituals, and reflects them back to her with its behaviour. Of course, this has to do with health habits and such, and as the transiting Moon sets off the natal Moon, her attention to clutter and space, in various dimensions, gets laid down in the habits of the child. Later on, the conditions of the workspace will be connected to the ebb and flow of emotional life. Daily rituals will provoke feelings of fullness and emptiness.

Those born with Moon in the **7th house** feel the power of their mother's relationship to her partner, husband, mate. The birth of this child coincides with her emotional awareness of him and their interaction. The infant connects physical and emotional nourishment rhythms with its mother's feeling of security within her marriage or partnership life. Later, marriage and partnership life will be the source of the deepest feelings of fulfilment and lack. For the Neptune in Libra generation, this often gets mixed up with a more rarefied spiritual longing. And for the Pluto in Libra generation, this human need becomes connected to issues of life and death and the generational need to transform partnership dynamics.

The Moon in the **8th house** registers most deeply the mother's fear of loss – loss of her partner, their security, and perhaps her fear of life, with its thread of endings, of death, as part of it. Also it registers her alternations of power and helplessness in the face of these things – her power to transform her marriage, her concerns about their security. Later relationships bring up these fears and the possibility of emotional transformations. Life itself is felt to be intense and powerful, and one with this position experiences surges of great power and feelings of deep abandonment. These people connect with others fully, or not at all. And transformation is part of their life experience.

With the Moon in the **9th house,** the mother is usually connected to people who are far away some of the time. The ebb and flow of the emotional bond is felt in relation to whether she is in contact with her own felt source – or that source is away. Of course, it can be that her own mother, family, or husband comes and goes, and she is secure and insecure accordingly. But I know someone with

Moon conjunct Neptune in Virgo in the 9th, and her mother was both religious and often ill. And the ebb and flow of security for the infant was connected to whether she was healthy and caring or ill and distracted. This person is in midlife now, and her security ebbs and flows depending on how deeply she is nourished by her religion – sometimes she feels the connection and sometimes it seems remote from her.

With the Moon in the **10th house,** your mother's attention to you is merged with her ambition. As the months go on, you register her attempts at perfect nurturing, both to fulfill your needs and to satisfy her need for respect from others. The work she does for your benefit gets set deeply in the layers of your emotional body, and you develop the connection between work and emotional satisfaction. When the work brings the respect you need, you feel nourished by life. When not, you feel starved of this source. And the ebb and flow connect you to the ebb and flow of life's abundance. It will be interesting to see how those who are born with 10th house Moons in the generation with Uranus and Neptune in Capricorn feel this. They are born into a time when the structures of social life are changing and reforming. Will these 10th house Moons feel their own personal rhythms of security and insecurity to be more dependent on larger issues? I suspect so.

With the Moon in the **11th house,** you register the mother's rhythms of attention in relation to her outside life, her group of friends and associates, her connection to her society's needs. Her own ideals for society, and how she engages with them influence you. Trust in the source of life is connected to your ability to connect with others in a meaningful way. You later find groups of people that are presumably working together for one or another ideal. Your sense of the fullness and emptiness of life is connected to collective ideals.

Audience: Moon in the 12th at last! We are always the last to be discussed.

Audience: Moon in Pisces is always the last.

Audience: I can hardly believe it – a competition for last place between Moon in the 12th and a Pisces Moon!

Audience: But I was impatient because I have Aries Moon in the 12th!

Darby: And where is your Pisces Moon?

Audience: In the 10th, but square Mars in Sagittarius.

Darby: Well, I'm glad not to have our ideas of Newtonian behaviour totally overturned today. Now we can all sign with relief, because our world is still operating within its own logic. So, on to the Moon in the **12th house.**

With the Moon in the 12th, your mother is in some ways deeply asleep during your early life. Possibly she is ill, in a hospital or institution, but it is just as possible that she feels secluded for some other reason. Hospitals and institutions are the obvious things, aren't they? I have a friend who had her first child at nearly forty. The child has the Moon in the 12th. And when I asked her if she was asleep in some way during his first few years, she laughed and said that she was desperate to get sleep, totally exhausted for his first few years, especially as she had her second child, unexpectedly, eigtheen months later! The Moon in the 12th registers its mother's inner soul life so deeply it sometimes hardly knows what it is feeling. Its deepest feelings are sometimes underwater for years. It is built for sacrifice and has a profound sense of aloneness which may or may not be problematical.

So, more words on some than others. But this is a one-day seminar and I can only give you what rises to the surface in the time I have. I'll have to do another day on the Moon to even get close to the fullness of this beautiful part of our solar system. Such a fertile symbol – but then it would be, wouldn't it?

The Moon will also show where you are most like other people, in the sense that your human foibles are most expressed. The house will tell where this common humanity expresses itself, where you are most at home. With the Moon in the 4th, when you are operating in your home and on your own patch, in your own territory, your natural responses are most ordinary. The sign and aspects describe your peculiar way of expressing this ordinary human behaviour. If you have Moon in the 2nd, in your need for material security, you are most like other people. So it is not only that you inherit something of that tendency from your ancestry, but it is where you specifically join the common herd.

CHAPTER 4

Lunar Aspects to Other Planets

*The Moirai or three parts of the Moon, representing birth, life and death.
430 BCE, Martin von Wagner Museum, Wurzburg*

Audience: I can see what you are saying about the houses and the attention given to the infant by the mother being felt against a particular background. But don't the aspects have a lot to do with it?

Darby: Yes, they do. Here is where the ebb-and-flow story becomes your own story. The aspects will describe, amongst other things of course, the duration and intensity of the emotional rhythm you shared with your mother. From one point of view, you are completely in effect, of her rhythm. But since you are born with this particular lunar configuration and it describes your personal emotional energy field, your energy also plays a part in the dance between you and others. And the aspects describe the peculiarity of the rhythm which later describes your natural emotional rhythm with other people.

ASPECTS TO THE OUTER PLANETS

Audience: What about the Moon conjunct Pluto in Leo?

Darby: Ok, let's start with something light! But first, let me say something about the Moon in strong aspect to one of the trans-Saturnians. We are looking at the aspects as the rhythm with which your mother nourishes you due to her internal or external circumstances. If an outer planet aspects your Moon, then for some reason your mother is feeling the power of the collective and responding to its pull and to you at the same time – particularly if it is a conjunction. In some ways, she is so perfectly identified with a particular dimension of the collective that often you are relating to a mother who is almost an archetype of something. Her personal life is taken over by this larger principle, either because she is so fragmented or because she is so exalted, and probably both at the same time. With tense aspects, the collective dimension is connected to her mothering of you, but in a more awkward and conscious way. With smoother aspects, these dimensions feed into her mothering but do not depersonalise it so completely.

How many of you have Moon in close aspect, of any kind, to the transpersonals? Almost all of you, from your show of hands. Well that makes sense in a room full of people studying psychological astrology – shall we broaden it out and say modern astrology? You probably all know that feeling of being possessed, exalted, taken over, or identified with something greater than yourself – whether through meditation or love, or eating chocolate, or through being on a magical or hellish holiday. And it's always through your intimate relationship life. You know what it is to be absolutely one with whatever it is that you are doing, and in that state, time disappears. You also you also know what it feels like to fall out of that state. Life doesn't allow you, as a creature, to be identified with something transcendental all the time.

We have myths about people who are masters or enlightened, and perhaps it is possible on this plane to achieve that. We hope so and wish so – either mastery or enlightenment, or some version of it. In a sense, that is when your creatureness and the transcendent state become one. But more often than not, unless you have done year after year, day after day, hour after hour of Saturnian work to earn that state, more often there is something slightly disturbing in it, and pathological, and your friends say, "Ha, he is in love again!" or, "He's off again!" or, "Inflation!" or, "Crazy!" Saturn is the gateway to those states. The state isn't actually allowed, except through Saturn's door.

Audience: Are you saying this was not possible before the discovery of the trans-Saturnians? And that it is not possible for those without such aspects?

Darby: No, no! Moon in strong aspect to Jupiter can make you identified completely with the Teacher, or Mystic, for example, and the Moon with Venus, the Lover. But with the outer planets, the identification is with something emerging into consciousness, still uncharted, planetary. Moon-Jupiter and Moon-Neptune both have almost religious experiences in emotional experiences. But they are different. The dimensions, shall we say, are different. Jupiter's territory has been charted since the beginning of astrology. Neptune's territory is new, and part of the development towards the unification of our species. Oh I'm getting into territory that is farther out than I wish to.

With Moon-Jupiter, you can become identified with a religious archetype, and you absorbed this from your mother's behaviour. But with Moon-Neptune you absorb something emerging – perhaps the traces of a collective reaching for the eternal, that is not fully emerged yet. It's more confusing perhaps, because we seek, find, connect with and lose our feeling of emotional fulfillment through something so elusive, so subtle, so as yet undefinable. The outer planets are still beyond our conscious reach. All the gods are beyond our conscious reach of course – that is their nature – but the trans-Saturnians reflect something that is beyond our collective sense of space-time reality. Oh, dear, I'm going to stop this now.

So, unless your mother was from another dimension, and you have the Moon conjunct Uranus, Neptune or Pluto, chances are there was something very disturbing going on in your early days. She was both personal and collective. She was the Dr. Spock mother, for good or for ill – the Moon conjunct Uranus. She was the lost and found, disappearing dream-mother – the Moon conjunct Neptune.

And with the Moon conjunct Pluto, she was the life-giving, death-giving Kali-mother. Her intensity in her motherhood was so great that, each time you received her mother's milk, you also received a charge of that particular state, and so either you go for enlightenment or you are a mess. There is not much leeway. At least it can feel like that. It is not only conjunctions that feel that way, it feels like everything-or-bust if you have any outer planet in aspect to your Moon. You either go for the highest manifestation of that planet, or you are suffering – one or the other. When it is conjunct, you may spend a lot of time identified with that planet and lost, because of that. Emotions have to be so powerful and so transforming, so spiritual and so enlightening, so exciting, or they aren't worth having.

With Moon-Pluto aspects, the intensity of feeling in the mother conveyed itself to the child. She was experiencing such strong emotions during pregnancy and the early life of the child that she had to shut down in some way. And yet the child with this aspect feels the intensity – he or she has receivers for it – and experiences mother, life, as very intense. Sometimes feelings are so intense they seem to get knocked out for a while. For those with the Moon in strong connection to Pluto, the intensity of gaze or feeling between mother and child is at times almost overwhelming. The mother's feelings are so strong and the child is receptive to being blasted. People with the Moon in strong aspect to Pluto need strong emotional interactions to feel anything at all. The life story as told by the soul is a powerful one. Events are felt intensely into experience or not felt at all. The soul is taken underground for periods of time, and nothing shows on the surface. Then there is an eruption and a sense of great intensification of emotional life. Then all is silent again, while the underworld goes on processing.

Audience: Persephone.

Darby: Yes, and Demeter and Hades.

Audience: Would it feel different depending on whether you have any brothers or sisters? If you have a brother or sister who has some other combination, at least you can vicariously experience some different side of your mother.

Darby: That's an interesting thought.

Audience: When I did my brother's chart, I was very surprised he had Moon-Pluto. I thought, "That was happening when I was little, in my house".

Darby: What do we mean when we say, "Our mother?" Where is this common mother? Recently I had a client who had Moon in Sagittarius square Saturn in Leo, and after he told me how cold and horrid his mother was, I asked, "And how does your sister get on with your mother?" "Oh well, she doesn't see any of this, of course, she thinks she's fun." I looked up the sister's day of birth and both the Moon and Venus were in Sagittarius that day, and they were trine Pluto.

Darby: But let me ask you, was your brother younger?

Audience: Yes.

Darby: Much younger?

Audience: Two years.

Darby: You were too young to know what was happening between them.

Audience: All I know is that I refused to come home after he was born. I had been sent to stay with my grandparents.

Darby: That is interesting in itself isn't it? That disappearance thing with the Moon.

Audience: You know, when you were talking about the transpersonals and master or mess, I thought of someone I know. He has Moon-Pluto very tight and he is a millionaire, and so he has really done the Pluto power thing really effectively. But I think it is really a less productive use of it. And yet, in his relationships, he strives for the other Plutonic experience – not so much the power, but the absolute intensity of experience, and very Plutonic kinds of experience. In one way he is a master, but in another he does get into some pretty messy experiences.

Darby: I think that is the case in general. We live various sides of the aspects. I suppose for us, the work is to recognise when we are in one or the other. We develop the power of reflection, perhaps as a result of the experiences that are constellated through our progressed Moon's passage. Through this power of reflection we can witness ourselves and our behaviour patterns. We can discover the possibilities inherent in our lunar position and configurations, and reflect through life on the sorts of things that happen to us. We can recognise our creature needs and how they express themselves through the sign, house, and aspects, and perhaps keep track as we go along, of ourselves and our damaging behaviour. We can't change the aspects – which represent certain givens in us – given with the gift of life itself. But we can see through ourselves over time, and get to recognise how our rhythms of fullness and emptiness express themselves. We can say, with Moon-Pluto aspects, "Here I am in life-or-death feelings in this money merger, or this love affair. I feel as though I am about to be transformed or killed – this is the way I engage with life."

ASPECTS TO THE PERSONAL PLANETS

When the Moon is conjunct Saturn or Jupiter, then whatever the social situation is in your home, and whatever social situation your mother is attached to, whatever social archetype she is caught in, you get it. You could say Jupiter and Saturn tell you about the local time-space gods, the authority figures. Saturn conjunct the Moon in Aries: Beleaguered warrior marries Amazon. Saturn conjunct Moon in Libra: the Judge of Fair Dealings marries Love. She is wedded to a particular social archetype, and you absorb the duties of that form with your milk. With Jupiter it is probably more fun. Your mother is confluent with the more adventurous, optimistic aspects of the social climate. Sometimes this is a pretty wild aspect. I have two clients with it who are on permanent medical drugs to keep them emotionally steady. But I also have a friend with this combo in Taurus, who goes over the top but never over so far she gets lost to view. When life is fun, there is no greater fun. And when it isn't, it is hard.

Moon-Venus conjunctions are known for having a very close relationship with the mother, though I often have clients who deny this. But from what I have seen, I think it is true. "Close" does not always mean "enjoyable".

Let me tell you about a man with Moon conjunct Mars in Sagittarius on the Ascendant. His main memory of his mother is frightening. He remembers being frightened by her, twice. He was around three when she died. He knows from the older siblings that she had many faces, but by the time he was born she was very distressed and frightened herself. He told me about one of the incidents. He was nearly asleep and she came in and grabbed him out of bed and made him say his prayers, as he had gone to sleep before saying them. He didn't know all his prayers, and she was very angry with him. He was very little at the time. As she died when he was so young, I imagine she was struggling for her survival at that particular time and trying to get over it. So she was all action and all movement and all anger.

Audience: Do you know how she died?

Darby: She "accidentally" killed herself.

Audience: That's terrible.

Darby: Horrible and sad and awful. He is Cancerian, and he speaks of her with love but remembers her with fear. He has Sun in the 7th house and the Moon on the Ascendant and he connects with people very powerfully, but in a specific way. He is extremely funny, and very philosophical, and is either absolutely on or pretty off, and silent.

When there are powerful planets aspecting the Moon, or let's say, rather powerful aspects to your Moon, then your mother is sometimes, often, intermittently but significantly, lost to something else. That is the main key of it. With the square and opposition, it can seem more like circumstances, but it is still her response to these circumstances. And because it is in your chart, it is your birthright in a sometimes odd kind of way – your existence brings the response out of her. When it is a conjunction, it is what she is most identified with at the time, to the extent of sometimes not responding creature to creature.

So if it is Saturn or Uranus, she is going by the book, whether the book is her social group or the book is Dr Spock. If it is Venus or Neptune, she is going according to some kind of romantic image, whether that image is taken from reading, watching television, or billboards of what the mother-woman is. It is very unconscious. So you absorb that, and then, in your own self-development, from crea-turehood to human, that is the energy you are working with. And it is passed on, exchanged between you in her gaze.

Audience: What do you mean by gaze?

Darby: That extraordinary look that transpires between mother and baby, again and again. It usually happens during breast feeding. It is a silent ecstatic communion that I have seen so often between infant and mother. Of course, there are mothers who cannot breast feed for one or another reason. But it still happens, with feeding and at other times. Some mothers allow it or have time for it a lot – often with the first child there is more time – other mothers have less time. But whenever it happens, it seems to be something which passes between the soul of the mother – which is part of the soul of her family, which is part of the very Soul of the World – and this new infant creature who will grow its own soul out of that past. Now, the aspects seem to describe the duration, intensity, and rhythm of that gaze, and all the shared time between infant and child.

There is a point at which it no longer matters whether the as-pects to your Moon are positive/negative, harsh/easy – it doesn't matter. There has got to be a point where it truly no longer matters, in the sense that you come to terms with who you are, reflected by whatever aspects. But we have to go quite a long way before most of us get to that point. And having struggled with all the issues re-flected by the aspects brings a finer clarity to your eventual self-acceptance. Looking at your early conditioning through the mir-ror of the Moon is a way to start, a way to proceed, to the kind of self-knowing self-acceptance that leads you to engage with life more wholly, less conditionally. There is a point at which any aspect and any placement simply reflects your entrance and early formation in life – your inheritance for better or worse. You as a human being are being built, building yourself, out of the circumstances that you inherited in your childhood

Audience: What about damage? So many of us feel damaged, particularly in our emotional lives. Or we think other people are, even if we think we're all right. Doesn't that come from our relationships with our mothers?

Audience: And our fathers!

Darby: Yes.

Audience: Is that the whole of your answer?

Darby: No, I thought I'd just pause there and see what happened. But I'll go on if you like. Of course, what we call damage comes from our fathers too, and from our environment, physical and psychical. It is part of being alive here. We have an ideal self, an ideal world, and we have what is happening to us here and now. And so often there is a huge gap. We have to deal with that gap. Here, we are looking at it through the Moon. We usually describe our own emotional difficulties in terms of the aspects to our Moon, and, of course, to Venus. It's rare for someone to think, "All my problems stem from my Moon in…", whatever sign it be. We will say, "I suffer because I felt abandoned with Moon in the 8th," or, "My mother's ambition for me has constrained me." But mostly we look to the aspects to understand why our emotional life is less than perfect.

Audience: I have Moon in Leo in the 2nd, squared Saturn in Scorpio in the 5th. I love my mother very much, and don't feel resentment towards her. I do towards my father, who I think is very cruel and has suppressed her terribly. But I admire her – and as you said about the 2nd house. I share her love of beauty. She has an extraordinary garden.

Darby: Ok. I can't help wondering if there may not be some sort of buried resentment, there with Saturn in Scorpio that may show up in some hidden way, or perhaps a hidden fear – but I do understand your deep affection for her, with the Moon in Leo and in the 2nd, and your pride in her creation. A Leo Moon loves to feel love, and hates to feel dislike or shame of those it loves. At some point, you may want to explore your inner world for signs of hidden tangles that may impede your own creative life. But I'm not suggesting you rip your psyche apart to find the secret pocket of lurking darkness. Just attend to the projections in your emotional life. It's something we all must do. And with the Moon square Saturn, one's attention to character development and one's emotional development are tightly linked. The Moon square Saturn has to work hard to stay in touch with the nourishment it gets and gives in emotional life. It can dry out, without noticing. It gets isolated. Do you ever feel isolated?

Audience: I'm an Aries. Do you think I give myself time to notice?

Darby: No. I guess you don't. Maybe it becomes physical.

Audience: My skin and hair get terribly dry.

Darby: Then perhaps it would be interesting to notice when you are uncomfortably dry as a possible sign that your inner life is too dry. It may be a signal that you have cut yourself off from the emotional flow around you. When the Moon square Saturn goes unconscious around these things, life gets very dry. Duty and responsibility take the place of warmth and comfort. Work hard and don't feel the feelings! The Moon square Saturn incarnated to a mother who was burdened and struggling with life. She was cut off from her own emotional needs.

Audience: In this case she had no time as she had two young children already and a violent husband.

Darby: And you absorbed that information from her every touch. The tendency to disregard your own feeling life coincides with the inclination to be very busy, so that you will not fall into feeling cut off. The part of yourself that judges, tows the line, works towards mastery of yourself – the Saturnian part – can be suppressive rather than supportive, to your emotional interaction with others, with life. You inherited from your mother a habit of self-suppression which was so deep she may not have even recognised it. Her natural instinct to enjoy her pregnancy, and the delight of her infant child, were counterweighted by a message deep within her to resist the sensual pull of this experience.

Audience: But I think it was exhaustion and the unsupportive attitude of my father, rather than anything in her.

Darby: Ah, yes, I do seem to be putting the emphasis on a suppressive message deep within her rather than in her circumstances. I think it's because you said the aspect was from Leo to Scorpio and is therefore a fixed square, that I felt it to be part of her nature, rather than simply circumstantial. But you are feeling your Leo Moon as her, and the Saturn as your father. It is very tempting to look at the whole chart here, and in some ways I should, but I want to stay as tight to the aspect itself as I can.

Whether it was ingrained or circumstantial, you absorbed that package into your body and emotional nature. You took that on with incarnation – part of the package. Often there is resentment and criticism of one's mother with this aspect, because she did not seem to support you as she "should" have. Perhaps this is more common with men who have the aspect, simply because … well, for many reasons. In your case, you feel sympathetic for her struggle with suppression. You might remember her harshness to you as necessary, considering her circumstances. But you are also harsh with yourself in response to your emotional needs. Are you hard on other women?

Audience: You mean women who do not live up to their responsibilities?

Darby: Yes, women who follow their feelings instead of their duties.

Audience: Well, I think it is very selfish to just do what you feel, of course. That's part of the breakdown in marriages, isn't it?

Audience: I think the "breakdown in marriages" as you call it has more to do with women having been suppressed for so long and now they are finding that they must follow their feelings or the world will continue to self-destruct.

Darby: And you have Moon in what aspect to Uranus?

Audience: Yes, well, I have it in the 10th house square Uranus in the 7th.

Darby: Interesting, isn't it, how we discover that our attitudes to how other people ought to behave springs out of this most fertile planet. What I am leading to here is that you have picked up your emotional body through your mother, and it is through her body that you absorb the events of your life that become your emotional story and lead to the development of your soul. In absorbing this from her, you are taking on that particular field of your family's emotional karma, the beauty and damage of this family's plot. Not all of it – just this chord, or strain, or pattern of pathology. Each child picks up its own chord, which it will learn to play from the womb.

And it goes into life with this chord, playing it over and over, and it will interact with others from this chord.

Audience: One of the things you were saying before is that the damage done to the mother gets passed on.

"THE PROBLEM WITH MOTHER"

Darby: Damage, yes. Let's use that word for that which impedes our natural ebb-and-flow response to the nourishment life offers in all its depth and range. Let's call this section, "the problem with mother." It makes me think of Howard (Sasportas). He used to love to put these kinds of phrases up, in his own particular ironic style. I think I will write it on the board.

What I am saying is, the damage – that which we interpret as damage – is part of the package of being born into this world. We each contain a personal and collective idea of safety and unconditional love, and this idea is mixed up with everything that is born of Earth and time. The wider the gap between this idea and what happens from day to day, the more it feels like damage. And there is no place more powerful than in our relationships with our mothers. For some reason, this is true of modern 20th century people. It would be interesting to go into the legacy of the last two or three thousand years, which underpins this new twist on the difficulty between the male and the female. But for now we have to remember that there is a long, complex legacy which probably comes out of Iron Age thinking. For us, it focuses on our relationship with our mother, and how near or far she was from the ideal that informs us individually and collectively. Unless your Moon is in Cancer in the 4th or in Taurus in the 2nd trine Jupiter in Cancer, you are probably going to feel damaged by the early relationship with your mother.

Audience: And probably even then!

Darby: Well, maybe not, because you are busy getting on with natural life. However, because the collective feels damaged by its past, its mothers, its parents, if you have any contact with the outside you will pick up the idea somewhere – through any outer planet activity. In a sense, there is hardly any position which doesn't show some kind of gap. The mother is the carrier of the goddess archetype. She gets it because we don't have any feminine divinity left. Some Catholics have the Virgin Mary, and if you have her enough, then you are less likely to blame the mother for all your ills. But most of us don't have the church or the religion, gods or goddesses on whom we can fasten our archetypal minds, so when it comes to the perfect, ideal, divine feminine principle, we look to our mothers in our particular 20th century Western way and she has to fail.

We have asked our own individual human creature mother to live the archetype. Furthermore, those of you who have children are expecting that your children are going to ask that of you as well. Whether they will or not is another thing. They might be doing something else completely, and not do that at all. But we have been doing it for a great part of this century. And as psychological astrologers, we look at the Moon, and its position and aspects, to see how we might describe the damage – the gap between perfect nurturing and how she behaved.

Someone said something about trines and sextiles. Why is it so hard to talk about trines and sextiles, and so easy to talk about squares and oppositions?

Audience: The lack of friction.

Darby: Yes. Talk about trines and you start sliding down. You don't have to become conscious of the forces interplaying with sextiles and trines. Maybe you do a little bit with sextiles, because you use them better, but less with trines because with trines it is given. So people with trines can't understand why everybody doesn't realise how simple it is, because all they have to do is this and then it will happen. Squares are all about work, because the development of consciousness is required with squares. Otherwise you just beat your head up against the same wall, or other people's walls forever. With lunar aspects, emotional situations activate mother complexes. But it is clearer, easier to see them, to get a grip on them with the hard aspects, isn't it? With the softer aspects it seems so right that you can't really grip it.

Audience: I have Moon trine Neptune and I get accused of being too merged with other people's problems. In therapy, that is a real issue. But I simply can't see why it is bad or wrong or anything not to be merged in that way. It seems as though that is how we should be with each other. And if there are problems with it, then they are better problems than not being able to identify with other people's pain.

Darby: And your mother?

Audience: She was very sensitive to me – later it felt like invasion. Later she became alcoholic too, when my father died. I thought my heart would break. But I would rather love like that, feel like that, than not feel.

Darby: Yes, I understand that. Your mother probably had a romantic image about what it was to be herself in relation to you, to her husband, and you absorbed that. But the romantic image did not interfere with your nurturing or the development of your sense of security.

What about Moon trine Mars? The mother is energetic, but the energy, as distinct from the square, doesn't cut across the making of your emotional rhythms. They come together in a way that feels right. They are connected. If you think of a Moon trine Mars or a Moon trine Venus woman, or if you think of it in a man's chart, and the sort of woman he will respond to, the Moon trine Mars woman will express her emotions more energetically and sometimes less gracefully than a Moon trine Venus woman. But they will be integrated into emotional life and not disturbing, not demanding consciousness and attention. There is not so much the feeling of damage.

Let me restate this. The sign in which the Moon is placed will tell you what version of the mother archetype you are attuned to. There are twelve different versions. I don't think the sign is ever a problem, because each sign has its own world, its own life. Perhaps it is more natural and comfortable to be in one sign rather than another, but the story of the Zodiac is that there are twelve major types, or possible manifestations, of any principle, any planet, and so Moon anywhere is simply one of the types through which the feminine side of life will manifest.

The house position starts to deepen the story. It tells what side of life kept getting triggered off over the first few months, and even years, of life, so that your attention was taken by that aspect of life in the ebb and flow of your early nurturing. The aspects from other planets either seem to either interfere or aid you in finding your way to life's nourishment. Aspects, and certainly to some extent house positions, say something about how your mother "damaged" you by not being able to live up to the archetypal image you had of her deep in the very notes of your body and psyche. The damage is that she wasn't the archetype itself, and aspects give you the pattern of how she deviated from that archetype. Of course, each individual astrologer will interpret the pattern from their own perspective – but the sign, house, and aspects will give the pattern.

And, to go one step further with this, the lunar pattern not only reveals information about the sort of damage, twist, or pathology, but it also reveals the pattern that points to your soul. It is that lunar configuration that tells you about your soul's path to growth in a fundamental way. So with this Moon square Saturn, you might look at your soul's journey as a journey in a somewhat harsh terrain – a journey that has deep pockets of isolation and silent beauty, and much work.

Audience: As I said before I don't feel that my mother damaged me, but I have begun to see that I can get very stuck on things. But usually I think it is because other people are doing things the wrong way. I am not sure about this in relation to my soul. I am interested in the way you are developing the relationship between mother and child and later development. I don't know about this word, though. But I am less afraid of isolation than I was when I was young. I don't expect relationships to save me from loneliness. I do probably work too hard to keep things out. I find what you are calling "eternity" when I am alone, certainly – if by that you mean when time seems to stop and everything is right. Working in the garden. Moon in the 2nd I guess.

Audience: Can you look at another aspect? Moon square Venus?

Darby: Yes – in what signs?

Audience: Moon in Taurus square Venus in Aquarius.

Darby: OK. So the archetype that you caught, picked up, inherited through your mother with Moon in Taurus is an earth mother, isn't it? She is the one who is in perfect rhythm, whose ebb and flow, whose waxing and waning has to do with being in contact with things around, in good contact with the earth, with her body, with your body. She passes on to you the sense, the possibility, the memory, the feel of good contactful earth. You grow in a womb that is really strong and connected.

But the way she styles herself, her particular style of movement of dressing, of self-regard, the way she regards herself and mirrors herself to other people is another sort of woman. Venus in Aquarius is far more intellectual, erratic, more "interesting", more people oriented, and so her particular way of interacting with others interferes with this capacity that you feel from her, her perfect ultimate nurturing. Moon square Venus people often go through life looking for a nourishment they never got. They did get it, but only enough for moments, and those moments felt so perfect, but they were never long enough – never fully satisfying because of that. There is the recognition of the possibility of perfect attunement to life, perfect comfort, and emotional situations set this off. But inevitably there is frustration, because if it is perfectly comfortable, then it is boring. If it is exciting, then it is too frenetic. One goes on, discontent and hungry. And that hunger and discontent often leads to collecting many different kinds of friends, and can lead to developing a very passionate relationship with life itself as the source of nurture and also the frustration of nurturing. It is a very personal relationship with life, with one's soul.

With Moon in Cancer or Moon in Taurus, when it – life, love, communion – is perfect for the three seconds or three minutes or one hour, it is so perfect, so complete. But with a square to Venus from either end, Leo or Aquarius, the mother's style of relating in-terferes with that perfect archetypal way. So one is constantly look-ing for that perfect nourishment – while relating in a way that is guaranteed not to get it, except for brief moments. Does that make sense? What I am saying is that the mother is not supposed to have given it in the first place. She is only supposed to give a memory trace of it, because no human being is there to satisfy our archetypal hunger. It is the archetypes, or what I am calling the archetypes – the gods, the transcendence or whatever it is, the shapes of things, what we used to call god and goddess and the divine – that is supposed to satisfy that hunger.

In a sense, with Moon square Venus, your very style of relating, as picked up from your mother, interferes with your ability to get the kind of emotional satisfaction you look for. There are moments that are perfect, but they never last long enough. This is later carried into other personal relationships. And yet it is this condition which offers the consciousness – this gap between the hunger and the real-ity – that leads to the questions which lead to one's own soul, and to a relationship with life, with one's life force.

As the lunar aspects reflect the internal or external things that interfered with a perfectly natural rhythm between you and your mother, so they give you clues about your own rhythms of relating to others, to life. The damage – that which twisted the natural rhythm out of shape – is that which describes our personal and intimate relating to ourselves, to others and to life itself. These are the rhythms with which we relate to our own source of being – that which interferes with, and which shows us the steps of our particular dance.

We are going to work with this way of contacting this source, this depth of life, for our whole lives. Let's look at one more dimension of this. Let's look at relationships with those who could become, or do become, our "significant others."

Our Moon is always activated when we are in physical contact with another. The more intimate the contact, the more the Moon and its aspects are activated. So, in a sense, all physical intimacy returns us to our source – our mothers, and through her, our relationship to life itself as expressed through our heritage. We feel most natural – even if natural is uncomfortable – with those who feel, smell, move, sound like our mother did to us as infants; not like our mother now, but who she might have felt to be in moments of intimacy. We say that men look for their mothers in their wives. They expect their women to be mother, even if they don't want them to be. There is some obvious truth in that, at this level. And women too need to feel some level of comfort and security with their male partners. And so the Moon comes in for us too.

Our natural rhythms of response and action must be acceptable to our partners – to ourselves first, and then to our partners. It is a natural instinct that, if you are in close physical intimate contact with another human being, your conditioned responses arise because the most intimate physical contact that you have in your life is the person whose body you came out of. You are in constant close physical contact unless the mother dies at birth – and that is a story in itself, told through your Moon – but you are never so close again to anyone else, unless it is a lover, or perhaps a nurse who is taking care of your body in illness, or in old age.

So anyone in those first few months, those first three years say, who is in absolutely intimate close relationship with your body, is conditioning you for any close intimate relationship you have later on.

When I first started studying astrology, I was in my twenties and we were all checking each other out, moving in and moving out with each other in Boston. We used to sit around looking at Venus and the Moon in the charts of the men we were currently interested in. Conversations like this would take place. "Oh no, he's got Moon in Capricorn trine Saturn. I'll never be able to do that for any length of time. I'm too airy!" "Yes, but you've got Moon in the 10th, won't that help? And look, he does have Uranus conjunct Venus in Gemini" "Yes, so he's attracted but it won't last when he find out I'm so heavy, with my strong Pluto." Or, "Oh look, he's got Moon conjunct Neptune in Libra! My Sun is conjunct Pluto, but sextile Neptune – he may be a bit too 'out there' for me in the end."

I remember it was quite a good exercise for us, because it was our way of talking about each other and learning at the same time. It gave us some silly notions too. I don't think it ever stopped us from following our feelings, or lusts or whatever. We probably didn't use the information properly at all, but we needed to be irreverent some of the time, I think. Our teachers were heavy into the spiritual side of astrology – we prayed to the Great Spirit before every class, and were made very aware of the awesome art that we were learning. So in off time, we played. "Oh, hi, who have you met?" "Well, he's got Venus in Sagittarius but Moon in Taurus squared Pluto – is that me?" Or, "He has Moon in Pisces." "Ah, alright, I'll go on reading Browning."

Audience: We do that, but it is more psychological. Sometimes it is a good thing for understanding the other person, but sometimes it gets in the way.

Darby: It certainly does. We interact with the aspect rather than communicating with the person, who is truly always an endless mystery under certain fixed behavioural patterns. But to get back to the theme. We are drawn to people by a certain inner recognition – a certain animal sense, very primitive, very deep. It seems to me we are drawn by our soul's need to commune with this other, and through the communion, to touch something – the source of life itself. Of course, nothing for we modern people is that simple or uncomplicated. We have to wade through mazes.

But let's look at it through the Moon. A man is attracted to a woman. There are many reasons, but the lunar story is that, if she can be described by your Moon, if she can come near the feeling of your Moon, then she speaks to you for more than a weekend. If she can't express herself within its field, she probably won't last more than a night, or a conversation. Perhaps if she fits too perfectly, it can't last – not for modern individuating adults. We are caught between, we who are no longer primitive, primarily instinctual, and we are not quite conscious yet. We are somewhere in between. We are not anything near our collective ideal – but we are no longer simply fate-driven. For people like us, if she fits it too perfectly something often happens. It just doesn't take for some reason, because it is almost as if we are not allowed to have the other person live out another part of ourselves too perfectly.

But if she can fit it a bit, enough so you recognise at some animal level her rhythm – if she fits it enough but doesn't quite fit it, that can work. For people who are in transition, as we are, that seems to be the thing that works best. She has to fit it enough so that you recognise her, so that you know what she is, what her fabric is. You recognise the weave, but she must not fit it perfectly. You have to be able to take back the projection. There has to be a gap. If she lives out your own soul perfectly, how can you find your own self? You never have a relationship with your own anima, in Jungian terms.

For a woman, it is slightly more secret, in the sense that she does live out the Moon and the rhythm, because a woman has to live closer to her body, just by nature of what happens to it through-out the months and years of her fertile years. Then somehow she lives closer to her Moon aspects, either unwillingly or willingly. And when she seeks a mate, she asks of him that he live out her Sun and Mars aspects – and a bit of Saturn thrown in on the side...

Audience: A bit?

Darby: Well it depends on your own relationship to Saturn and to Uranus, doesn't it? But equally, she asks that he be able to take her particular rhythms, that he be able to respond to her. Her Moon describes her capacity and range of adaptation to another – she is most comfortable when he can accept her rhythms. The rhythm she absorbed through her mother is hers, and she expects to be met in that way.

Audience: Can you give an example?

Darby: Yes. If you, as a woman, have Moon in Sagittarius, square to Jupiter, you are unlikely to be any kind of comfortable with a man who is absolutely Saturnian with a bit of Uranian thrown in. He has to let you be free in a particular way, free within the tribe, free within the convention. As a woman, you must be allowed to be Artemis. And if he has no Artemis in him, then no amount of common back-ground, intellect, or physical attraction will make for deep merging. I have to say that it is very unusual for lunar positions and aspects not to be reflected somehow between people who go any distance together. Sometimes you can meet under a progressed Moon aspect and get confused by that, but if you give it some time, the truth will emerge. We meet and mate so quickly these days – there is no time to let the true rhythms emerge really.

Audience: I have Moon square Neptune – what would that say about my expectations of women?

Darby: Yes, let's look at it from a man's lunar position. What signs?

Audience: In Leo square Neptune in Scorpio.

Darby: Mother as queen, good or bad queen, but queen, lost in the collective underworld journey. The collective atmosphere in her environment confusing her natural instincts. A lost queen. This would lead you to search for regal women, perhaps lost too, but perhaps poetic, romantic, extreme, soulful. Your soul develops through communion with these women, and through the disillusionment experienced through these women. Sorry, this is very cryptic, but I can only give an impression here, to express this train of thought.

Audience: It's fine. Just to tell you, my mother was an alcoholic, married to a very degenerate man, my father. She divorced him when I was around ten. She stopped drinking and developed a deep spirituality, which she still has. And the women I fall for are always lost queens, poetic, sometimes mad, sometimes extremely creative. My own spiritual quest, the finding of my own soul, has just begun. I still ask women to be her – but more and more I feel what you are calling "source" through the gaps.

Darby: Whew. OK. A man or a woman you have just met is probably most always a mirror for your projections. The more individuated and clearer they are, the quicker they break through your projections. If there is an emotional connection, then your Moon gets going, ready for action, for receiving and for giving, for being nourished and for being abandoned, for being picked up and put down according to the rhythm that is innate to you. If you have Moon and Uranus in sharp contrast, then your expectation and your natural behaviour will have an erratic, unpredictable rhythm. Either it will seem to come through the other person, or you will feel it towards them, and probably both. With Moon-Mercury aspects, you will flip between two levels of communication, which may not be consistent and may generate misunderstandings. But whatever the aspects, the Moon is yours and you better get to know it and to deal with your own and other people's problems with it, because it is the way you access your own soul, your connection between time and eternity.

The Moon is about waxing and waning, it is about ebb and flow, it is about reflection. It is the rhythm with which we expect to be picked up and put down. That expectation may not accord with our ideal of being picked up and put down, but it is our rhythm. You experience being put down, being told good-bye on the phone, leaving the party with the host yawning, and your having to leave the party has a kind of abandonment. It plucks the chord, and the Moon is those chords which go all the way into the core of your being. It not only operates within your relationship, it operates within your rhythm with life.

Now let's look at this waxing and waning and ebbing and flowing. We could say we have to be put down as well as picked up. We have to say good-bye as well as say hello. We have to be engaged with intimacy at whatever level our lunar nature can take intimacy, and at the same time we have to be left alone. If we are perfectly satisfied by others we can never develop a relationship with our own selves, our souls, our own connection with life. And so it is the moment of abandonment or loss, it is in that moment of rejection, that we need to be more attentive than at any other time to our process – either when we are rejecting another or when we are feeling rejected ourselves. If we don't feel rejected, either we are defending ourselves slightly too well, or we are suppressing it. I suppose that is the same thing. Our Moons show the kind of acceptance-rejection with which we interact in life, and life means other people. Sometimes I can feel rejected because it is raining when I wanted the Sun to shine, or when the bus doesn't come when I need it to.

Audience: You must feel rejected a lot in this country.

Darby: I have learned a lot about myself through being here. I can have an existential crisis almost any day of the year – especially when the bus doesn't come and it's raining.

Audience: That's a lot of existential crises.

Darby: Yes, I've noticed that English people are better at this sort of thing. I often seem to be the only one re-evaluating my own life and the nature of existence in the bus queue. But perhaps everyone else is doing it secretly, and I haven't learned that it's impolite to articulate it.

Audience: Do you actually express it?

Darby: Yes, I have to admit that I do. I either end up feeling like one of the "loonies" who walk the streets of London, or I have some really fine conversations in bus queues.

Audience: The joys of being foreign.

Darby: Absolutely. Now, what I have been saying is that there is something about the ebb and flow of the Moon in any emotional relationship, and in your response to life's experiences. Inevitably a person is going to come too close to you, and inevitably they are going to be walking away when you want them. When you go on holiday it is raining and you expected sunshine. That is life, and your Moon responds to that.

Your chart will tell you the style with which rejection comes, in its small or grand ways. If you have a Martial Moon and you ring a friend up who said she will be there at six and she isn't, or the phone is engaged, your anger will be immediate and the anger will pluck the chord that goes all the way down to the frustration of not getting what you wanted at six months old. If you have Venus-Moon and you go to a friend's house and the food is not as good as you expected and they don't offer you tea, or they are a bit offhand, the feeling of distress, the sense of not being loved enough, is easily set off. Let's stay with that scenario. If Moon is opposition Saturn, it will feel like you have been rejected because you aren't good enough or you have done something wrong. If Moon is square Mercury, perhaps you got the wrong day. With Moon-Jupiter, you bring so much food yourself that is unlikely to happen!

Audience: Or it's never good enough but you have fun anyway.

Darby: Yes.

Audience: What about Moon-Uranus?

Audience: You'll be shocked because you had such high expectations.

Audience: And you didn't even know you had those high expectations. What about Pluto?

Audience: You'll sweep the food off the table and leave forever?

Audience: No, more likely you'll not say anything...

Audience: ...But have an existential crisis on the way home!

Darby: So, you see, we are just looking at the different style of feeling situations which might set off the rejection chord in your feeling-memory system. I think it is really useful to watch those moments of rejection, especially if they pile up over a period of time, because they are the ones that signal that it is time to turn inwards and to go into your own inner life. This can be through your body – some people can connect to their emotional waves and rhythms through their body, through meditation, stillness, or through movement; dance. Others do it most easily through their imagination – again meditating, drawing, painting, active imagination work, attending daydreams. There are many ways. Some do it formally, through psychological awareness and the processes that generates. Others do it through routine tasks – washing the car, ironing, cleaning the attic, gardening. You know that contained feeling when you have settled yourself again after a series of knocks.

We are looking at it in terms of your relationship to life, and the Moon as it waxes and wanes. It's as if you got full out there and now you turn inward and return to yourself so that you can come out again, to return again. You have reached full and now it is time to wane, to bring yourself back to your body, back to your memories of what happened yesterday, of what happened last week, last year, of connecting this moment with early childhood memories. Because every time you are stopped in your tracks, there is an image of childhood that is right behind it. Every time you are going along from moment to moment and it is all working fine, and then suddenly something stops it, if you stop and look downwards, your childhood is sitting there. If you have an emotional reaction, most likely your childhood is moving right there under the surface. Your emotional reaction may be very muted or very intense, or somewhere in between, depending on lunar position and aspects. It may be, "Oh dear," or it may be, "Kill!" or it may be, "Sob." But over time you get to recognise it, if you pay any attention at all. And so over time you can begin to recognise it as familiar and it becomes something to attend and listen to. By attending to it, you can discover the key to turning the events of your experiences into food for the development of your soul.

Once again, we are looking at the Moon here as the symbol for your instinctive emotional relationship to life and to others. And we have been thinking about how you can recognise the turning of the tides, and so allow the ebb and the flow of your own particular rhythms to express themselves. We are trying to see how we can reach outwards and turn inwards according to our nature's rhythm, as described by our Moon and its configuration. We are looking at our ability to recognise ourselves in our personal ways of connecting to life. Our Moon expresses our commonality. It is where we are the same as everyone else through our needs, but it is also where we do this sameness differently.

So someone with Moon-Jupiter connects to all life through expansion into different species as well as different kinds of people, different tribes. Someone with Moon-Saturn connects to all life through its hard and thorny landscapes. Moon-Chiron connect through the wounds that open up through other people and through the wounds of life itself – the wounds of time-bound eternity. People with Moon-Neptune get nourishment from...

Audience: Pubs.

Darby: Pubs? I was going to say tears, but pubs might do for some.

Audience: I cry into my beer quite frequently.

Audience: And nature, and music.

Darby: Again through feelings of loss, through becoming invisible – let's put it that way – through knowing that it is sometimes absolutely perfectly appropriate to be merged with your environment. I know a few really good photographers with Moon square Neptune.

Audience: I have Moon square Neptune and opposing Uranus and when I am really upset, I can't do anything except wander round the streets that are really busy, because that is anonymous but there are still people.

Darby: It is not about relating to them is it?

Audience: Oh no. It's about just being lost in the crowd.

Darby: Whereas with Moon-Uranus it is – you have to actually relate to them. You have to make up excuses to relate to them, just to be part of the flow, and that is nourishment. Perhaps it is the Moon that can show us how to waste time – Saturn – because if you can waste time then you can use time. If you can't waste time, chances are you don't use time well. I say waste from Saturn's perspective, as opposed to from the Moon's – like to wander around the streets, or, if you are lucky enough to live close to nature, to wander the hills, or the fields.

Audience: What about Moon and Chiron? You haven't said anything about that at all?

Darby: I just did.

Audience: Yes you did. But not enough.

Darby: Feeling undernourished here? All right. The only thing I can really say that I know about Moon-Chiron aspects, particularly the hard aspects, is that they reflect the wounds that we are noticing in our relationship with the Earth itself, with the physical ground of our existence. The wounded relationship with one's own mother opens one up to something that is being acknowledged now, in our times. We have got into a hurtful relationship with our world. We cannot stop hurting nature, and nature seems to be hurting us back – our pollution, and our Earth's inability to protect us from the harsh rays of the Sun, for instance.

Those with Moon-Chiron aspects seem to be wounded in a way that reflects our collective woundedness. The inappropriate uses of food and sex, and the jagged rhythms of intimacy and aloneness, reflect our relationship to our own world. In whichever ways these aspects express themselves personally, they can always be linked to something collective and wounded. Moon-Chiron people reflect this collective sense of wounded species, wounded world. And their spiritual journeys, through their emotional woundedness, may help to lead us back to a new connection with our selves, our world.

Audience: What about adoption? Does that show up in Moon aspects?

Darby: I have to say that I don't know. I have a close friend who was adopted, and I have had several clients over time who were adopted, but I don't see anything that would indicate adoption in general. Astrology is frustrating like that, and reassuring like that. There will always be unknowns and mystery. I am sure somebody has done proper research on this, and probably knows what similarities there are in cases of adoption. The two women I know both have Moon-Venus difficulties – one a square between them and the other each planet squared by a transpersonal. But I don't know.

It would always be coincidental with awkward lunar aspects. My close friend who was adopted has Venus square Neptune and Moon in the 4th in Libra square Pluto in Cancer in the 12th. To be born out of one womb and then nurtured by another hand must have a profound effect on one's life. My friend is in her late 60s and lives by herself, and her soul connection to life is very powerful. She lived quite a wild emotional life and has settled down to something quite profound. So I know from my own experience that adoption does not stop or impede soul development. In a way, it is just another circumstance. And you find your way through it, or you don't, like any circumstance.

CHAPTER 5

Transits to the Moon

Inuit mask worn to embody the Moon

Audience: What about transits?

Darby: To the natal Moon?

Audience: Yes, as when Pluto opposes your natal Moon.

Darby: Let me just touch this, and then we'll stop. If the planet that transits your natal Moon is one that is part of your original lunar configuration, it will set off the configuration, which is reflecting your emotional habit – it will set it jingling. All your "stuff" will come up to be dealt with. It will give you another opportunity to feel back into time, down to your early beginnings, and deeper through your ancestry to your source. It will set off comfortable or uncomfortable patterns, according to its own logic, but it will pluck the chord through internal and usually external events. There is always a chance to reflect downwards and to choose to accept or reject your own life's story.

When the planet transiting has no original part in your lunar story, then it may reflect events, according to its own dynamic way of working, but it feels more like something that happens, rather than something that *happens*. It does not necessarily get turned into food for your soul. But there are always other things happening in your chart at the same time so this is just a kind of French grammar lesson.

Audience: French grammar lesson?

Darby: Yes: here is the rule, and there are as many exceptions as you can imagine. When it is an unaspected Moon, emotion is there, but it doesn't connect to anything else. It is as if it happens and if you are there when it happens, you know that person is emotional. But if you are not there, you have no idea that the person has had an emotional experience because it does not communicate itself emotionally. Emotions and soul contact with life are separated out from the other dimensions that make up a person. So it is almost as if, to develop your own soul, with an unaspected Moon, you have to be separated in some way from others. It is an aspect which would be good for meditating – where the person actually separates to connect with oneself, one's soul and all of life.

Audience: Liz talks about that as being a bit like having a tenant in the basement and, until you go down there you don't know they are there. You might suspect them, but you don't know they are really there until you go down.

Audience: Emotions pop up. They are not something you know. It is at its most primitive and mythic.

Darby: I have a friend with Moon conjunct Pluto in the 8th un-aspected. When she is in love – has a lover – she is intensely emotional in all situations. When it is over, she goes back to being quiet again. An unaspected Moon is a unique experience. The past is a closed book most of the time. Emotional life is very private, very separate. It can indicate an extraordinary connection to life, but it may seem rather impersonal to other people. It doesn't mean that there is not love, but love is a separate experience. It can be very lonely, but it can also be very holy, in a very private way.

I know that there are more questions arising – I can see them in your faces and feel them in the room. But I'm going to stop with the natal Moon here. I hope you will keep the questions in your minds and ask them later of yourselves and each other. I'd love to generate more questions than answers with this – I mean questions that you can't get rid of until you address them yourselves.

It's time for serious bodily nourishment now. Let's have lunch.

CHAPTER 6

The Progressed Moon

Painting by Luiz

Now I want to speak about the progressed Moon. It is the most interesting progression to follow simply because it goes around more quickly than any of the other planetary cycles – every two and a half years or so, it changes sign. In just under twenty-eight years it has gone around the whole of your chart and returns to its own place. This cycle reveals the unfolding story of your emotional development. The progressed Moon draws you onward, yet always returns you to your roots. It becomes a mirror in which you are invited to reflect on the nature of your own journey, as lived through your emotional responses to other people, but also to life itself. It is connected to the Saturn cycle and, over time, these two cycles can reveal to you the underlying pattern, the warp and weft of the tapestry of your life, lived in the midst of the infinite dimensions of life itself.

In the next Moon seminar, I shall talk about this interweaving cycle. But today I want to open up our imaginations to the progressed Moon through simply looking at it as it goes through the signs and houses. In this way we will begin to explore it as the mirror you can use for the development of your relationship with your soul. We'll start with a few keys, to unlock the doors to its secrets.

THE MOON AND SOUL-MAKING

Let me start by turning to James Hillman. Do you know his work? Most of you seem to be familiar with him, I see. You could say that he is a post-Jungian but that might be unfair to both men. He was certainly profoundly influenced by Jung, and in fact was a Jungian analyst until he became his own brand, so to speak. He's an Aries with Sun and Moon in Aries in the 11th, as far as I know, and he certainly has influenced collective thinking with his restless pioneering heart and soul. His books arrived at a time in my life when I was grappling with forming into thought my intuitions about the progressed Moon. The word "soul" has a lot of history for me – early Catholic education and all that. His writing helped me to bring my conditioned thinking into the present, and he helped me marry my religious imagination to my psychological awareness. Many of his ideas served as a launching pad for my own development of the ideas I am presenting to you now.

One of the most powerful insights he ever awoke in me came from his quoting a passage from Keats. Keats wrote a letter to his brother, in which he referred to this world as the "vale of soul making." He says that this is the use of the world. Hillman develops this idea of soul-making. And his work helped me to give mental form, to my intuitions about the progressed Moon.

He defines soul as that which makes meaning possible. He says that it is soul which – and I am quoting from *Re-Visioning Psychology* here – "turns events into experiences, is communicated in love, and has a religious concern." He goes on to say that soul deepens events into experience. He says that by the word soul, he means "the imaginative possibility in our natures, the experiencing through reflective speculation, dream, image and fantasy – that mode which recognises all realities as primarily symbolic or metaphorical."

I reflected long on that. This thing I call soul, that which connects me, in time, to something eternal, is part of, or fundamental to, my imagination. And it describes the space from which I reflect on the events of my life. Events occur, and it is this soul that digests them, reflects them, in such a way that they become my experiences. Undigested, unreflected events, do not become real experiences. This process of turning events into experiences happens through reflection on the images that rise out of the events in our lives. We think about these events through the images that arise out of them

Hillman has taken the word soul away from the exclusive realm of one or another formalised religion and he is saying that it is soul, it is the power of reflection, the imagination returning to events and re-visioning them, reconnecting with them, that is soul-making. The phrase soul-making is very evocative. There is an imaginal space in which something happens. I suppose I would say that, as we move towards that space, we come into relationship with that place where matter and spirit meet. We begin to inhabit that space between the visible and the invisible, between matter and spirit. Our lives are ensouled, deepened into both time and eternity through reflection.

So an event happens to you, but unless it happens in your imagination, it is not an event, it is not an experience. It is reflection that turns events into experience. And for astrologers, reflection and digestion have to do with the Moon. I want to repeat what Hillman says: "Soul turns events into experience, deepens events into experience. Soul is communicated in love and has a religious concern in that it is concerned with death." This last quality of soul returns us to Jung's idea of the Moon as the gathering place of departed souls, and to the Moon's role as focus for ancestor connection.

It is through the Moon that you remember your ancestors, that they remember you. Through this you are connected to not only your personal past, but to your deep past, which goes all the way back to the beginning of time. The past lives in you, and each new experience you have returns you to that past and brings that past into the present, which leads to your future. You connect yourself to life through your past, as absorbed through your mother's body and psyche in the womb, and later personalised through your experiences with her. And through your life, each new emotional experience deepens this connection with life, and through life to eternity.

Audience: Is Hillman writing directly about the Moon?

Darby: No – he is writing about soul. But I am giving you one or two of his ideas, because they were so helpful to me. I hope this is not confusing. Some of his ideas have become so much a part of my thinking that I don't even know where they come from anymore. *Re-Visioning Psychology* and *The Dream and the Underworld* are held together with sticky tape in my library. And, of course, I have absorbed his ideas to develop my own. Great authors give us that gift, the gift of inspiration.

He says, "Soul makes meaning possible; turns events into experience." It is the soul – that "part" of oneself we may call the soul – that makes meaning possible, because it is the soul that reflects. Nothing has significance unless it is reflected upon. Everything that has significance will be reflected upon. Now for us, as astrologers, it is the Moon in the chart that embodies this reflecting. If you have Moon in water or earth, by sign or house, it is perhaps more natural to reflect on the past. If you have Moon in fire or air, by sign or house, it is easier to imagine the future, to throw your soul forward. It is less natural to reflect on the past.

Oh, I've just remembered something. An image, a memory of Howard (Sasportas), has risen up in me after saying that. He had the Moon in Taurus. He connected me to our times when we were with each other, when we were in our early twenties. With his Moon in Taurus in the 4th house, he never stopped referring to everything that happened to us in earlier times. We spoke of them in London, brought them up to our present life. He remembered things I had forgotten, but he brought them back to me. We reminded each other of more and more things, and wove our original story into colours that illuminated both our personal tapestries. Had I not come to London, he would have been part of a piece of my past that continued somewhere else, and may or may not have ever been remembered. I came to London, connected with him, and through his Moon in Taurus he reconnected me to my past. Our emotional connection in the past was brought into our present.

Audience: Did his Moon connect to anything in your chart?

Darby: Yes it did, to my Venus, and my Mercury in the 9th house. We were reconnected in a foreign country, as well. My Moon conjoined his Venus. So we could return each other well – and happily. Hillman's statement that soul deepens events into experiences is the key of this section. Through reflection, events are turned into experience. And experience has meaning, and leads to meaning. A life of events has no meaning. Think of Jupiter's exultation in Cancer. There are many ways of reading that, and one of the ways is that you find meaning through reflecting on your past. By reflecting on your experience, by having that as part of your life, your life connects up – the dots of events are joined into something that makes a pattern, and that pattern reveals meaning.

Audience: Are you saying that there is an ultimate meaning to life, and this process which you are describing discovers that meaning?

Darby: Good question. Hard question to answer properly. I am saying that this thing that I am calling soul is the meeting point between matter and spirit, between the visible and the invisible, between the temporal and the eternal. When you engage with this part of yourself, you attend it and its power of reflection, which is its nature. This place of living refection, this soul, by being attended to, does what is natural to it – it serves to keep you alive to time and eternity. It mediates between time and eternity, and in doing that, it discerns patterns in your life, which are reflected in nature, and which connect you to nature – patterns which manifest in time but reveal the invisible realm we call spirit – which returns you back to time. And through this a sense of meaning arises.

Audience: Um…Could you, I mean…

Darby: Yes, hard to articulate. Let me put it in astrological language. The Moon stands for your mother. But your mother had a mother who had a mother – all the way back to the beginning of time, of matter, of manifest reality. The Moon describes aspects of your mother and your early mothering, but it goes deeper than that. Through the habit patterns of relating to your body and your life and to others, you are re-minded of your mother, and that takes you to your deeper past, beyond your own personal mother and life.

Now, the progressed Moon goes around. From the moment you are born, it is separating from itself, so to speak, and taking you into your own life. Your past, your deep past, absorbed through your mother's body, is brought into the present and reinforced and particularised by the interactions between you and your mother. This is revealed through the aspects and houses that are associated with your Moon. Habits of relating are set.

But your progressed Moon is telling you that you are also being drawn towards relating in other ways to other people. Yes, your natal Moon is constantly being reinforced by emotional experiences, but you are also being drawn by the future into new experiences. Going back to observe your own life through tracking the progressed Moon and the experiences that arise from its contemplation, and noticing where it is now, and observing your emotional life from its images, ensouls your life.

The patterns you begin to discern lead you to reflect, and this reflection leads you to deeper reflection. The Moon is always going round, always moving from one point to another. By tracking it and staying in touch with it, you have to keep moving too. Patterns unfold and cannot be turned into fixed dogma about life if you keep abreast – a good Moon word – of your own inner changes in perspective. You reflect from this soul place and your reflection keeps you alive to life's changing constancy. This soul-making, and I think I would rather call it soul-relationship-making – making a relationship with this reflective part of yourself – keeps the process of reflection and discernment of meaning alive. The events of your life are constantly being digested into experience and each new day brings something more.

Life has meaning when you begin to perceive a rhythm, a pattern in your daily life. It takes on meaning. Jupiter is exalted in Cancer. In the ebb and flow of daily life we find meaning, if we give ourselves time to reflect on it. So through reflection, events are turned into experience, and experience leads to a sense of meaning. I am not saying there is A Meaning and you find it; I am saying that the search for meaning is part of being human, and pattern perception is natural to humanity. Pattern recognition leads to meaning, and these meanings are often turned to dogma, which then stop one from further development. We are looking at ways to keep moving, stay alive to things here.

Audience: This word "meaning"…

Darby: Mean, middle, but also from man and mind. And it is a word which signifies thinking and, in fact, signifies signification, significance.

Now, the progressed Moon: You start with your Moon somewhere, anywhere, with the Moon in any aspect. You are born and you are brought out of your mother's body and into external contact with her body. From the moment you are born, you are being drawn away from your personal mother through gathering the events of your life into experiences which become more and more your own. At first it is barely noticeable, and after a month of life the progressed Moon is only 1° away; just the sliverest tiny bit away, and the following month it is a little bit farther. It is hardly noticeable – not really noticeable until it is about 15° away, or 30° away. 30° is about thirty months, which is about two and a half years old. Once it is 30° away, and you are two and a half years old, then it has made some kind of contact with every planet in your chart.

Audience: That is the same amount of time Saturn takes in a sign – at two and a half Saturn will have covered the same amount of territory. It will also have touched every planet for the first time.

Darby: That's right, and I will talk about the link between the progressed Moon and the Saturn cycle next time. For now let's just remember that they are always in close relationship with each other – though over a full lifetime they slowly move apart, which is interesting in itself. Content and form slowly separate, or at least develop a new sort of relationship. But let's leave that for now. For the first twenty-eight years they move pretty much apace – they keep the relationship they have at birth through their cycles. This is more obvious and probably more significant if they have a real relationship in the natal chart – I mean if they are in aspect to each other, or in mutual reception, or in each other's house. Someone with Saturn in the 4th will feel the weight of his or her past shift and change as the progressed Moon goes round and opens up new sources of nourishment. Someone with Moon in the 10th will redefine their relationship to their work, status or position each time Saturn changes sign and house.

Audience: And their relationship with their mother and her ambition for them?

Darby: Nice one, yes. New aspects of character development, new relationship to life's necessary duties, will reverberate down the chord that demands a remembering of mother's ambitions for her child. The nourishment received and given through work or social position, the times of hunger and feelings of poverty that arise because of position in the world, will be reworked each time Saturn moves sign and house. Both the progressed Moon and the Saturn cycle reflect aspects of separation, reorientation and reconnection with life at the next stage.

But let's go back to looking at the lunar side on its own. Where the Moon begins describes what you and your mother share, in terms of the heredity you have both come from. You incarnate through her, and you are the next possibility of that lunar heritage. That lunar heritage carries on, that heritage of that family habit pattern carries on one more step, but at the beginning she and you are so close – hardly a breath between you. Then, every breath you take, the progressed Moon moves away, and so you are moving away from her. She is still conditioning you, but you are moving away from her.

THE PROGRESSED MOON IN THE SIGNS

I want to simply go round the signs and then the houses, and so in doing this, I have to take a leap here. Except for those of you with Aries-Moon, the progressed Moon will enter Aries some time after you are born.

Audience: But we are last to experience it consciously.

Darby: True. You have Aries-Moon, and so you experience everything from that emotional vantage-point, but oddly enough you don't get to experience it until latest of all, at your lunar return around your twenty-eighth year – which is also the leadup to your Saturn return. Those with Pisces rising will not experience Aries until just before their first Saturn return. Those with Libra rising will experience Aries at around fourteen or so. But whenever it is, that is a beginning.

When the progressed Moon goes into **Aries**, you begin a new cycle. It is different from Moon going into the 1st house. When the Moon progresses into the 1st house, the beginning is very personal, because, unless you have Aries rising, it is in another sign, and that sign describes the way you, personally, enter life. It is your particular vehicle for getting around – your persona, your filter, your armour, your calling card, your mask. It is where you enter the field, the way you both show and cover yourself. So it also describes a new phase of your life, a connection between your personal way of interacting with life and your emotional rhythms, emotional ways. It is as if your persona gets ensouled, connected to your inner life. Your past and present connect in your personality expression.

When the progressed Moon goes into Aries, and that sign is in another part of your chart, you have about two and a half years to experience as much as you can, what it might feel like to be Arian – brave, heroic, driven, self-propelling, hunting, seeking, action.

Audience: Selfish, angry, demanding…

Darby: Yes, thoughtless, impatient, rushing out into life. This is your time to experience what that energy feels like. Of course it will be modified by the house it is in and the aspect it makes, to your natal Moon particularly. You cannot be full-on Aries unless you have planets there. But you get as close to feeling this rush, this impetus, as you possibly can. It is really "sperm energy." It is where you take off in flight, are shot out of the canon and aiming for connection and birth. You connect with the initial rush of something-out-of-nothing that is the birth of creation.

The first time the progressed Moon reaches Aries, you may be more out of control than the second time, nearly thirty years later. The rush of self-propelling is there, but you have more power to reflect because you have had many years of experience behind you. But the rush will be there even if you're ninety. You will feel the urge to leap forth, and the more you can leap, the better it is. When your progressed Moon is in Aries, to try and be contemplative and quiet is really against the grain somehow. It just doesn't work. And anyone who got to know you when your progressed Moon was in Pisces might find you a bit sharp to the bite, so to speak!

Once the Moon moves into **Taurus** there is a settling in. That which was initiated in Aries now seeks to take root. Your soul is developing whatever capacity you have for steadiness and dogged persistence. The house and planets touched will tell you more about the sort of internal and external events that are connected to this sense of rooting yourself into something.

The first time my progressed Moon went into Taurus, I fell in love with trees. I got obsessed with trees, obsessed by them. Because I have such happy planets in Taurus, it never went away, but it was quite a love affair at the time. Taurus may be uncomfortable for those who have an awkward relationship to their bodies, or to sensual pleasure, but it does draw you towards nature in a big way. You have the time to feel as close to the beauty of the earth and the earthly as possible.

Audience: Are possessiveness and jealousy part of it?

Darby: Possessiveness and your capacity for deep attachment, and maybe jealousy, that depends on other things, I think. You make something yours, during this time. What began as an impulse in Aries, becomes yours in Taurus.

Once your progressed Moon moves into **Gemini,** everything splits apart. Again, this is comfortable or uncomfortable, depending on your natal Moon. And the events of it depend on other things – transits, other progressions and the Moon's natal condition. But here is where you get to talk to your soul. You find there are two of you. One is in time and one is somewhere else, and they must converse. You may be cut off and fragmented some of the time, but you also get to communicate with a side of yourself, or other people, that was not available to you before. You experience the sense of duality in whichever house Gemini lives.

Audience: Or two houses.

Darby: Yes, do you have Gemini across two houses?

Audience: Yes, and my progressed Moon is just crossing the line between the 7th and the 8th.

Darby: Well you might find the conversations you enjoyed before get a bit pale. You might need to talk to people on a deeper level now.

Audience: I've really been enjoying parties for the first time in my life, but last week I went to one and I was so bored. Now I think it may be that I was looking for another kind of connection.

Audience: In the 8th, I wonder what it might have been?

Audience: Oh, I see. Well it's funny you should mention it but there were some pretty sexy women there that I hadn't registered before.

Darby: Hmm, with your progressed Moon in Gemini, and in the 8th, you might have some pretty exotic conversations for a while.

Audience: I'll have to warn my partner.

Darby: Yes, though some of them might be with her. The progressed Moon in Gemini lets one into some of the finer secrets of conversation, with others and with oneself. One is split and one converses to make whole that which feels split.

When it moves into **Cancer** there is a descent into feelings that can be uncomfortable for airy or fiery people. One discovers the need or the capacity for self-containment and nesting.

I must say I have never met a woman with progressed Moon in Cancer – if she is in the child bearing years – who does not get broody for a time. For women who have not been cut off from their creature instincts, it is time to have babies, for those who can. It is very hard to resist the pull of that ancient demand of the life force. Also, any natural need for security that has not been addressed comes up.

Audience: My progressed Moon is in Cancer in the 7th and I am feeling absurdly possessive of my husband. I have Moon in Aries and Venus in Gemini, and I am not like that at all. The other day I cried because he went away for the weekend with some of his male friends. I felt so abandoned! I couldn't believe it, and neither could he. He has never seen me like this. And that broody thing – it keeps coming up.

Darby: Ebbing and flowing. But keep track of those feelings. They may be awkward and uncomfortable, but if you can navigate those waters, you might find a closeness that you have not known about before. You are connecting to all the women who feel this way about their mates, and all the men who get clingy with their women, and I'm sure you have not tolerated them before.

Audience: That's an understatement. I am feeling like the wimp I thought I'd never be. What's good about that? My husband is mostly fire and air too.

Darby: From the soul's perspective it is not a good thing to be un-connected to feelings and life experiences. To be cut off from others, because we judge them from our own narrow perspective, is against the Moon's wisdom, which ebbs and flows and sheds its forgiving light on everything. To be fed by life's abundance, to be part of the Soul of the World, to be really connected to life's deep source, we have to feel everything that it is to be human. Feeling dependent and needing protection and wanting to be part of the family, are human. Some people have more of it than others. You are having it now. It may lead you to a deep feeling of oneness with a part of humanity that you have been cut off from – and it may lead you to the kind of emotional intimacy that you will treasure forever. But you may have to explain to your husband that this will only last a while, if you're not to frighten his fiery nature. Also, make sure you know where his progressed Moon is, so you can keep track of each other.

Audience: I think it may be in Virgo.

Darby: Then he can work with that. Each lunar progression has its own beauty and its own disturbing side. And the ebb and flow story applies all the time. Each position brings you its fullness and its dry-ness. You are most secure and contained in Cancer time, and most neglected and cut off. It is experiencing these rhythms that connect you to the rhythms of life on Earth. Trying to "fix" yourself in the good feelings keeps you slightly mad.

Let's move on to **Leo**. Wherever Leo falls in your chart tells you where the light at the heart of your spirit finds its way through – or you might say, which area of life is illuminated by the life-force. Suddenly I want to call the Sun the life-force, and the Moon the life-source. Words are so impossible. They both reveal and hide things at the same time; they illuminate and confuse

Audience: Hermes.

Audience: Trickster.

Darby: Yes, magic and charlatanry. Anyway, the house lorded over by Leo is different, of course, to the Sun's house, unless you have Sun in Leo in the 5th. The house where Leo rules is connected to the Sun's house by a subtle link – like the king's summer palace. So when the progressed Moon goes into Leo, the summer palace gets lit up and ready for guests. The queen is in attendance. And your soul connects to all the regal, proud, arrogant, exemplary, dominating, resentful and leaderly ancestors in your heritage.

Audience: Resentful and leaderly?

Darby: Yes, I think one of the difficulties of Leo Moon is its resentment that, well, that it is not the Sun, I suppose. Or something like that. It has so many fine qualities, but it carries this expectation which our onward-into-Aquarius world does not give opportunity for.

When the Moon progresses into Leo there is an expectation of something splendid. And when life is splendid, it is grand. But when the lights are out and it is grey and dreary – the ebb of the tide – there is a feeling of outrage that I have noticed. Those who have the planets amenable to expressing anger and outrage find an outlet, but those who don't wander around liked exiled royalty.

I am thinking of a Scorpio friend whose Moon went through Leo recently – through his 10th house. When his work dried up, as it did periodically, he was almost confused, hurt. He didn't have the nature to express anger and outrage, and so he simply looked a bit tatty and lost – like he'd been wearing golden robes and they got spattered by rain. When it is shining – I mean life and the connection with people that one loves or admires – then, oh, what a splendid time! Magical. You are connected to the big IT. But when the palace is shut and dark, lost egos wander the streets. We know what it feels like to be displaced royalty. A good experience in this country, don't you think? A bit of sympathy for that lot?

Audience: Are you a royalist?

Darby: Probably. No, I'm a romantic.

Audience: Leo planets, then?

Darby: It's a secret.

Audience: In the 12th or the 8th?

Darby: Shall we go on with our work?

Audience: We might as well, we're about to go into Virgo.

Darby: And so we are. The progressed **Virgo** Moon is a bit of a shock after the Leo Moon. For some it is restful. For others, too gritty. My Scorpio friend said, when his progressed Moon when into Virgo, still in the 10th, "I feel so much better now, not so exposed." He got on with his work, which suited him, as his Sun was in the 6th too. Virgo time is time when you get to sort things out, whether you like it or not. The house Virgo rules – and you understand I mean where Virgo lives – is where you have to keep track of the details anyway. But also, this is your time to connect to that part of your ancestry where those who were in service to life lived. You discover the joys and the endless small tasks of your service to life. Anything that interferes with your getting on with things, irritates. You tend your garden – whatever part of life is your garden. The ebb and flow of daily life activate the part of your soul which is sensitive to any kind of pollution. You feel things acutely and react with nervous intensity to any whiff of criticism. You are as close to a craftsperson as you can get, depending on other things. This is where you craft life, and its joys and upsets are reflected in your body and soul.

 Libra is a time of balancing. The house where Libra lives is where you must find and lose, and find balance, again and again. The

Moon progressing through Libra opens you up to beauty and truth and their weave. Your soul seeks to find its point of balance, and through finding it and losing it and finding it again, you discover a place within yourself where your poise is most needed, and most enjoyed. Ugliness – what you find ugly – hurts, and you are most selfish and most generous in your attention to beauty and grace. Those who are graceful draw you towards them. Those who are crude or raw repel you. And those sides of your nature are drawn out and drawn in. Relationships, especially partnerships, demand a fine balance from you and a grace that is natural or unnatural to you, depending on other things. It is a time where your soul discovers its capacity for compromise.

Moving from Libra to **Scorpio** can feel like moving from the beach to the ocean – and I am not talking about the Mediterranean here. I am talking more about the Atlantic Ocean, which in my experience is pretty wild. It is a time of intense feelings, and the house where Scorpio reigns, is the house where tumult lives. Confrontation and purification are part of this house's experience for you. Any dishonesty with yourself is paid for by a darkening of the light. Your deepest fears and your experience of power are brought out by relationships and by the events of your life, which are reflected by transits and other progressions. You go through the storm, and those of you who like storms feel most alive here, on the edge. It is a place where you live on the edge, in the sense that this house activates your capacity to feel abandoned and your ability to regenerate no matter what. You come out of this progressed Moon time with a feeling of profound clarity and a sense of your own power. But this power is given by life itself, in which we live and die and live and finally die. And at some point in this time you are confronted with that.

And then the progressed Moon moves into **Sagittarius**. And oh, it felt like a party to me. For some, it is too diffuse of course. And for those whose imaginations are dominated by their intellects, it is sometimes chaotic. Your imagination rises up with all the force of a high wind. The house it inhabits tells you where your imagination fires you to move into the future with as much faith and optimism as exists in your character. This is a place of restless energy, and it lifts you up into realms of possibility. And, of course, it casts you down from the mountain top of your hubris. But what adventures you can go on! And how significant things appear to be. Your emotional nature is open to sensing patterns everywhere – and it must be a very awkward time if your fixed stand-point is that there is no meaning. But that can become meaningful.

The Moon progresses into **Capricorn** and what has been fired into images that have significance for you in Sagittarius, begin to take shape in the depths of your nature. For those of you who are engaged in true work, this is an absolutely wonderful time. It may be lonely – many people have felt the isolation of the bare mountain landscape of it inside, but it is where any capacity for disciplined effort towards a goal becomes part of your nourishment.

Audience: What do you mean by that? Disciplined effort may lead to nourishment, but it can't be nourishment itself.

Darby: Yes, I know what you mean, I think. Capricorn is opposite Cancer, and so it should be an uncomfortable place for the progressed Moon. But that is not my experience so far – at least not with adults. Two of my long-term clients have told me that when it went into Capricorn in their early teens it was incredibly lonely. One of them lost her mother, and she had to take over her role a bit with all the younger children. The other lost all his friends, for some reason which he cannot remember or never understood, and he spent all his time playing with math puzzles. Yes, he did become a mathematician.

He came to me during the second passage of the progressed Moon through Capricorn, and it was lonely again, not as extreme, but different this time because of maturity and knowing about it. When it went into Aquarius and over his ascendant, he burst forth with the most incredible conception, which has been feeding him and his colleagues for years now. And his family, of course, because it turned into something quietly lucrative. The loneliness might have been the 12th house too.

The point here is that the experiences that you have of loneliness and focus, responsibility and burden, and development of mastery, in one or another area of life, are drawn together by this Moon and become part of your soul life. Living with the reflective possibility of the progressed Moon in Capricorn during this time gives you the mirror in which you are able to reflect on the manifest realities of life. What I mean is, you get as close to being on a bare mountain, alone, or responsible for others, and this gives you the capacity for understanding this part of reality. It's "the buck stops here" part of the cycle.

Audience: And what did you mean by true work?

Darby: Did I use that phrase? True work is that which you do with all of yourself. You give yourself to it, heart and soul. And you are usually recognised for it, though it does not have to be paid employment. I have a friend who is literally a housewife – that old-fashioned vocation which is a bit out of fashion. She loves her husband and family and her house. She is a master housekeeper, and yet because she does it out of love, you don't feel you can't sit down anywhere in her house. It's not hysterical housekeeping – it's natural somehow. She loves her work – and that work is keeping house for her family. Very unusual in my circle of friends and acquaintances! When her progressed Moon went into Capricorn, I thought she'd want to go out and get a job or something. She did have a moment of thinking that, but then she decided to reorganise the cellar and the attic and she ended up having a bigger house by doing that. I watched in amazement.

Each progressed Moon moves you into another step in the round of life. Each one is individualised by where it is in your chart and how conditioned it is by transits and other progressions, but

THE PROGRESSED MOON   101

each one, each sign, moves you inexorably from one facet of life to another. And as your soul reflects, so you deepen into life. On some level, we are always grabbing and rejecting – we are creatureness after all – but in your soul life, you have the power of reflection, and this is what you use to turn the events of your life into your experiences which connect you to life's source.

The Moon's movement from Capricorn to **Aquarius** is not usually as noticeable as other changes, maybe because of the Saturn connection between the two signs – unless, of course, you have a planet right there at 0° or 1° Aquarius. For a time, it might seem to continue the Saturn theme. But eventually you notice it is less controllable. Whatever house is tenanted by Aquarius is the area of life where you cannot follow conventional procedures, isn't it? You might want to, you might try, depending on how strong your Saturn is, but you really can't. And so, when your progressed Moon goes there, you are chopped and changed a bit. The nourishment of it is the variety of experience. And the hunger of it is for everything at once. The experiences your soul registers during this time are so varied, and reflection is fragmented. But you get as close as you can to experiencing what it is to be versions of yourself that you have not been much up to now. This phase awakens the parts of you that other phases cannot reach. Through reflection, your soul awakens to its uniqueness and its sameness. You join the club, so to speak – some club, any club that carries a version of your ideals.

The slide into progressed Moon in **Pisces** is slower than some. The house tenanted by Pisces is your melting point anyway, isn't it? Oddly enough, or maybe not oddly, this can seem a rather extreme time. The good feelings are really magic and the bad feelings are really rain-forever bad. You might say that your soul is drawing together all the unresolved, uncompleted emotional experiences of your life so far, and they are settled into your being, becoming both forever yours and diffusing back to forever. We can't talk about Pisces without poetry, but let's try to be factual. Pisces can be very sad and very happy. Disillusionment and loss of ego positions are the paths to nourishment. The more you give, the less time you have to brood. But brooding may be the best way, sometimes, to deepen into life and to bear the truth of final dissolution. Let's stop here.

I know that, by running through the signs like this, I open the door to all sorts of frustrations, because anyone can say, "Yes but when my progressed Moon was in Pisces I got a new job and had my teeth out and what's that got to do with Pisces?" And we can run through all the, "But where was your Saturn, and how was it aspecting this or that, and what house and aspect is this or that in?" And on and on. What I am trying to do here is to give you an imaginative possibility with which to access that part of you which is reflected by the progressed Moon. Once you get the image, or images, which are reflecting that part of you, then you can go there any time during any stage of it, and reflect your life into your own soul's dimension.

This morning I was talking about the natal Moon sign as something that is developed during your time in the womb, something that carries your ancestral habits – the chord in your ancestry that forms the basis of your own emotional development. And this chord is your personal way of emotionally engaging with other people and life experiences. The house and aspects further define it and personalise it, but the sign is the chord.

Now, when the Moon progresses along, you might say that it plucks the chords that you did not choose to follow – chords you did not follow all the way to birth. But all ways of being are in us. We all go back to the very birth of the universe, so everything is there somewhere, and when your Moon moves from sign to sign you are able to touch something beyond yourself for a while. And by touching every way of being, you can eventually be in a deeper way. I don't think using your progressed Moon to reflect on your life in this way gives you any more happiness or peace or comfort, or fixes anything at all. It does make you sit more completely in the place between your creatureness and your divinity, between your beast and your angel. That's all.

Have any of you been working with your progressed Moon? What do you know about it?

Audience: I know that my progressed Moon is in Scorpio. The thing to watch out for is that you get a kick from it during the actual moment when the progressed Moon enters a sign. Then it settles down, and you absorb the energy. But when it first goes into that sign, you meet somebody, something happens which says, "Progressed Moon changed sign." It happened to me on the minute.

Darby: But I know you, and you are a person who operates to the minute! You can tell us what happens when it goes into Sagittarius. For me, it takes a few weeks or even months to register the change. But I am more of an impressionist and you are more of a fine etcher. With the Moon, I like working with the layers of things. The Moon progressed into Scorpio is different from its movement through the 8th house or when it is in major relationship to natal or transiting Pluto. They all activate the depths, but in different ways and with different results. So there are multiple layers to the Progressed Moon.

In a sense, the progressed Moon points to the place where life is poking at your relationship pathology, revealed through the natal Moon. It does so from different angles, in different ways, as it moves along. If you have the Moon in the 8th, and you are particularly sensitive to rejection by abandonment, then each new phase of the progressed Moon will set that off at some point in its own particular way.

Audience: You get a chance to feel abandoned from twelve different perspectives!

Darby: And each time, you get the chance to address it from a new perspective, or to reinforce your old feelings and ideas about it. But it also lets you into other ways of being human. When the Moon is in Gemini, it allows you to connect at the level of gossip. You might have Moon in Virgo in the 10th and never gossip because it seems inappropriate behaviour. But when the progressed Moon goes into Gemini, if you don't gossip, you are wasting a perfect opportunity! Gossip is one aspect of the wind that flows between us. You can choose the level on which you do it. The urge to connect with others, and with an unknown part of yourself, is strong in a particular way now.

Audience: You mean you can finally tell everyone all those awful secrets you have about the people in your government office?

Darby: I think I'm heading for a law suit here. I can see the tabloid headline: "Astrologer told her to do it." And my progressed Moon is in the 7th at the moment.

Audience: Whatever you say now will come back to haunt you once it goes into the 8h.

Darby: I'm getting paranoid in advance.

Audience: When my progressed Moon went into Cancer, I don't remember feeling that I wanted a child, but I did buy a lot of plants for my house. Also, it was the first time I ever lived alone, and I loved it.

Darby: When your progressed Moon is in Cancer, you may not want to have a child, but it is phenomenal how many women start getting broody at the end of progressed Moon in Gemini. But for those of you who do not connect with the ancient natural urges of cave, family, tribal continuity, still this very deep part of being human will express itself somehow. By watching the "how," you reflect your personal life into the greater life.

When the progressed Moon goes into Leo, if you don't find yourself bragging a bit, you are wasting a perfectly good opportunity, and that means that when it is in another sign and you find other people bragging, you are going to put them down. You might do that anyway, but if you have reflected on your feelings during your Leo time, you are more likely to understand that urge, deep inside. If, by the age of seventy, we don't have some kind of tolerance, we have wasted huge chunks of our lives. It is the progressed Moon that offers us the opportunity to become more of a human being. If you went through two and a half years of really feeling full of yourself and then being deflated, and then getting full of yourself, and then getting deflated, when you see someone else doing it, you are not going to be intolerant of that, you can't be. But I don't know if that is really even the most important thing about using your progressed Moon, to reflect your inner orientation. Well, maybe it is, come to think of it.

Audience: What is the other thing, that either is or isn't more or less important?

Darby: Well asked! The two things I am seeing here are the Moon's reflection of the ebb and flow of feelings, outwards towards others and inward towards yourself. Neither is more or less important than the other. Feelings ebb and flow – that is their nature, as it is the nature of bodies of water on this earth. Each sign the Moon progresses through has its own orientation, its own way of constellating events into experience. The events, inner and outer, are reflected through transits and other progressions. The Moon draws them together, through feeling, into experiences.

You can get in touch with those inner dimensions, those feelings, through attending the progressed Moon, through keeping an eye on it. Your natal Moon gives you information about the emotional patterns taken on simply through being born. The progressed Moon can keep you up to date and moving emotionally, intertwining the past and its habits and experiences with the present and its abundance and emptiness – by acting as a mirror in which your life is reflected. The sign and house it is going through gives you the dimensions of the mirror.

On a lighter note, I have noticed that one's style changes as you move from one sign to another. This is maybe more particularly for women than men. When your progressed Moon changes sign, you change your style. So be careful. When the progressed Moon is at the end of a sign, don't get caught by the sales. I have had that experience.

Audience: What sales?

Darby: Well I was thinking of clothes sales. But it might be anything, of course. I have noticed that, if I buy something at the end of one sign, I might regret it by the time I have caught up with the next sign, inside myself.

Audience: (Male:) I never change my style of dressing – I've been wearing these same jeans for more than ten years.

Audience: We've noticed!

Darby: As I said, this may be more for women than men – but men who express themselves through their clothes and their colours might notice it as well. And women who don't, won't.

Audience: So you shouldn't buy a house when the progressed Moon is in Gemini, because you might not like the neighbourhood once it's in Cancer?

Darby: Hmm. I'm not sure this is the sort of thing I want to encourage here. I don't want to advocate using it so practically. There is something else here. It's that if you begin to pay attention to the things that are drawing out your emotional reactions within the field of the sign your progressed Moon is in, you get a feeling for something. You track your inner life in a certain way. I didn't mean to distract you by such a concrete example, and I don't want you to make rules like that for yourself. I have just noticed over time that my style is modified by whatever lunar progression I am experiencing. Perhaps that is because I express my emotions through my clothes, and so it speaks to me that way. If you express your emotions through your home, then you're likely to change it, or change it around every time you move signs. It's more like that. It's about noticing what expresses your feelings, and paying attention to the possible changes as you come to the end of one sign and move into another sign and its world.

Audience: My progressed Moon has been in Scorpio for nearly two years now. All during that period, my mother has had a Pluto square.

Darby: So both of you can share that at some level, in the things you are talking about and the things you are able to access – if you are able to share at all.

Audience: Luckily we are.

Darby: This reminds me to return to mother for a moment. As you enter each successive sign, there is a shift in your interaction with her too. I think these are more noticeable in the lunar progression cycle, which I will talk about another time, next seminar – when your progressed Moon squares your natal Moon, opposes it, etc. But I think it is worth watching each successive sign too, for new sides of your relationship to her. It is also worth knowing where her progressed Moon is, and the relationship between yours and hers. I have a friend whose Moon and his mother's were square at birth. And they had a hard time until he was in his late twenties. By then, their progressed Moons had come into trine to each other and their relationship has improved over the years. It can work the other way, too. Your relationship can get more and more, shall we say, challenging, over the years. Check to see if there is an awkward Moon-Moon progression between you.

Audience: I seem to change relationships every two or three years. That's a bit scary – it might be every time my progressed Moon changes signs!

Darby: Check it out. It does seem a bit extreme.

Audience: I don't change friends when my progressed Moon changes signs, or partners, actually. But I notice I re-evaluate every friendship that I have. I've been following it for about ten years now.

Darby: That makes sense. And speaking of partners, it's a good thing to keep track of your partner's Moon and yours. I've noticed that people with whom you have progressed Moon sextile are the friendliest sort of connections. There is less tension, more interest than any of the others. Of course, the progressed Moon opposition is probably the most interesting, but demands care and attention to what flows between you. Trines are fine, of course. And squares are squares, of course! I have a close friend with whom I am in progressed Moon square progressed Moon territory. Our Moons are natally unrelated. I am fascinated by how we endlessly have to almost translate what each is saying to the other about people, relationships, life. The Moon always operates most noticeably in your most intimate relationships. And, of course, it is a way of keeping clarity about your children's emotional development. It makes more sense of some of the things that can be confusing. But again, I'll say more about that in the seminar on the progressed Moon cycle.

THE PROGRESSED MOON IN THE HOUSES

Let's go on to houses now. Again, these are just notes and clues and images to get you noticing things.

I have noticed that, in the early years of one's life, the progressed Moon going from house to house brings you experiences that happen directly through your mother. She is focused there, in that house's territory, and so you go with her. Every seven or so years you shift another step away from her into inhabiting your own life – though some of us hold onto our pasts more than others, consciously or unconsciously. I'm not even sure we can do much about that – the soul has its own time really. Sometimes I think we can only attend – reflect, watch, think, and attend.

When the progressed Moon leaves the 12th house and enters the **1st house,** it is truly like a birth. You and your emotional body connect. You feel yourself more directly. Whatever sign rules the Ascendant is your lead-in to life, and when the progressed Moon goes into that sign, if it is in the 12th, the rumblings of an awakening begin, but usually still hidden in your dream life. Once it goes over the Ascendant, your need for self-reflection becomes strong. All through the 1st house, the tendency to self-reflect ebbs and flows, and you need to do things that emotionally satisfy your image of yourself, or nourish your image of yourself.

As the progressed Moon goes into the **2nd house,** this self-reflection turns toward your natural resources. The sign tells you something about your general attitude and capacity to generate these resources. Planets in that house tell you what parts of yourself engage with their development, amongst other things. But now, here, you engage with these resources very personally. Through reflection, your natural talents come alive.

Audience: And you feel strongly about money and things?

Darby: That may be. If you are three years old, you will not so much reflect on things as feel very possessive of them. When the Moon returns at thirty-one or so, by then you have had time to reflect on this instinct, and through reflection to deepen your experience of being resourceful, in whichever ways you are. The ebb and flow of your emotional life shows up as satisfaction and dissatisfaction with your material circumstances, certainly. You feel safe and unsafe with your capacity to generate security. But it is the time for reflections on your own bounty and the bounty of life itself. This is what makes the feelings of this time constellate into experiences that deepen your sense of living on the earth.

Going into the **3rd house** connects you to your mental environment and yes, to brothers and sister and neighbours and such, in one way or another. Experiences with these people ebb and flow between nourishing and unsatisfying. Conversations which do not nourish your mind are really unsatisfying. Emotional connection is made with people who can nourish your mind. You are hungry for information, and it will depend on your natal Mercury, and the sign ruling this house, as to how you deal with this. Natural information junkies, beware! Hermes is a trickster as well as a magician. But if you pay attention, and reflect on your experiences during this time, you will discover the kind of information that nourishes you, and your natural way of accessing it.

When the progressed Moon goes into the **4th house** there is a deep turning inward. Even if it is in a fire or air sign, and you restlessly run around, something in you is seeking deep connection with, not only your own emotional life, but your very roots. Feelings run deep, and the emotional experiences of this time pluck the chords that take you back to your family, yes, but far beyond. The images that rise out of this time can bring you into present time perhaps more than any other house, because, if attended to, they profoundly settle something about time and space as your house, with eternity as your home. And yes, the ebb and flow shows up as contentment and discontent with the way things are – your home, your country, your father, your self.

In the **5th house** it is harder not to have fun than it is to have fun.

Audience: What if you have Saturn conjunct Neptune there, square Venus?

Darby: Oh alright – no. I think I shall insist on my right to give you my perceptions, as I am the one standing up here today. Maybe fun is not something everyone values, or even has. But if you have any capacity for it, it's here that it will show up. Let's be more accurate. This is the house of creativity, in the sense of children, paintings, poems and songs. What is fun to you may not be to someone else. It is a time when your emotional life centres around the children of your body and your mind. Whatever sign and planets are there will circumscribe and channel this innate need to create something. When you are having fun it is great, but the ebb tide takes away the fun of self-expression and then you can feel very lost in the playroom.

Audience: Could this be the secret Leo coming out?

Darby: This is Leo's natural house, after all. I'm being perfectly objective – sort of. The imagination rises and falls strongly in this house when the Moon is passing through. And when you feel you are expressing yourself it feels good. And when not, not.

Audience: I have Moon in Taurus in the 2nd house. When I was six, and my progressed Moon went into the 5th, my mother put me in a school that was noted for its creativity. I hated it. I have Saturn in Leo in the 5th. When the progressed Moon came round recently to the 5th house, I started painting. It's hard going, but it feels right, good.

Darby: That's interesting. I have noticed that the second time around is easier all around – but perhaps that is because of the natural maturing process. For those who do *not* enjoy the process of reflection that maturity brings, because of its demand for re-evaluation of one's own, often odious, behaviour, the second time or third times are less enjoyable. Everyone has different experiences. But it's this reflection I am trying to foster – it is telling your story through the progressed Moon, telling your life through its stages, and reflecting your life so that in the end you experience your life in a way that connects you to all life.

If you live primarily in your body and feelings, then you are deeply connected to life. If you live in your imagination and your mind, then you have the power of observation, but may be unconnected to others or to the Earth in a feeling way. If you use the reflective light that is available to you then, the two are connected, because you move from fire to earth to air to water continually through your life. You live them all. It's mad to miss it.

Onwards to the **6th house.**

Audience: Back to work again?

Darby: Is this a lunar *deja vu*? As your Moon moves into the 6th house, any neurotic symptoms that are habitual get set off. I mean any habits that are automatic reactions, rather than responses to present time. Your sense of order and control, ebb and flow. The sign, and therefore house ruler, tells you something about this. Planets there focus your attention again and again.

The 6th house tells you what sort of gardener you are. The 2nd tells you what your garden grows. And the 10th, how you bring it to its full potential in time. But the 6th tells you about yourself between the two. And so, when the progressed Moon goes into that house, you emotionally connect with that garden-shed part of yourself, and feel the urge to sort it out and rearrange the tools and figure out what is possible.

Audience: And the health side of the house?

Darby: Yes, well, you are gardener to your own body in the first instance. And the progressed Moon here will connect you to that too. Health issues that come up during this time, expressed by transits and other progressions, are more closely connected with your emotional life than at other times. No, that isn't quite the right way of saying it. Your emotional needs may be expressed more directly through your body with the Moon in the 6th, and this has the power to lead you to find ways of working to bring body and mind into better communication with each other. If you are fine around all that, then you will be urged, from within, to develop more satisfying work rituals.

Your satisfaction with your work space and your tools, internal or external, ebb and flow, but in such a way that you are more likely to adjust them to suit your present needs. Your soul takes nourishment from rituals that make your life work better. Clearing out and ordering your world, internal and external – getting better nurturing for yourself when ill or distressed, either from yourself or others – is part of this passage, which brings you to a recognition of what must be continually attended to. This is the repair shop of your life, and something is always being brought in – and that will always be so, as long as you are alive. This Moon progression gets you to inhabit that space.

The **7th house** is another of those turning points. It's a time when, may I say, you give your soul away. Or other people see you wearing it, and they take it for a while.

Audience: To have a soul you must lose it?

Darby: I was thinking something like that. We know from psychology that when we fall in love, we fall in love with ourselves in the other – at least in part. I saw an old movie from the 1930s recently, and a character said something like, "Oh the usual story, they met and immediately both fell in love with themselves." I laughed out loud. With progressed Moon going through this house I think your soul flies out of yourself to another, or others, and you run to find it. Of course, it depends on the sign – more likely in water or fire, probably. The ebb and flow of this Moon definitely has to do with feeling nourished or starved in your relationship life. It gets you to notice others in a way you might not have up to now. But you also might chase shadows.

Whatever is begun in the 7th gets profoundly challenged in the **8th house.** Dressed in ball clothes in the 7th; naked in the 8th. Tumble wash time. The past rises up like ghosts. All your past relationships return to haunt you, and ghosts are laid by the dozen, or not. You are fulfilled and abandoned by others, hungry and sated with contact. The sign on the door of this house is your way in, but once in, the process is the same – tumble washed until all the impurities rise to the surface and are flushed out. And this is always deeper than just your personal past. Ancestors who live through you – mostly active if you have planets in this house – get to speak to or through you. And you resolve things that are deep in the habit patterns of sex and money matings in your family. The part of you that dwells between time and eternity gets thrown back and forth between the two here, and you connect emotionally with life and death in a way that changes your perspective, usually quite radically.

And then, in the **9th house,** you come out of the marshes into the mountains, slowly or quickly, depending on you and the signs involved. We all have a mountaintop in us, and the sign on the cusp tells you the nature of your mountaintop place. The obvious 9th house things, like a natural longing for travel, get activated here, because your emotional needs and your need for going beyond the known world come together. I would always keep an eye on your method to uncovering meaning – using the sign on the cusp as the entrance to the dimension in yourself where events turn into experiences and experiences are shaped into patterns that feel significant; that makes meaning. Your Moon going through the 9th gives you a foreigner's eye. The ebb and flow give a feeling of fullness and emptiness around this. Being a foreigner is exciting because you see everything with a strange eye. But it is also tiring, because being without your tribe does strange things to your imagination – wonderful things, but strange things. I think you connect, as a soul, past and future here. Your soul connects to meaning, mission, truth, in one form or another. Reflection embodies this into your way of relating.

Once your progressed Moon enters the **10th house,** that meaning, mission, is thrown against the mountain to see if it has any purpose or useful possibility. The progressed Moon in the 10th brings your emotions to your work in the world. Any natural need you have to manifest something that will be recognised as useful or valuable to your community is ensouled here. The ebb and flow show themselves in feelings of acceptance and rejection of your need for respect and recognition as a person of value. You are drawn to people whom you feel can further your path to mastery of one thing or another. Some of these people can, and others simply show you your limitations. That's the hard part. For those with a strong sense of purpose and discipline, this is a very fruitful time.

I saw a client recently who has the natal Moon in Taurus in the 8th and her progressed Moon is in Cancer in the 10th. She came to me upset because she suddenly feels that her job no longer reflects her sense of herself. She said, "It's died on me." And although she has felt this on and off over the years, this time, it seemed appropriate to do something about it. So we spent time looking at her transits, to see when she might open out to new possibilities. She has always kept her job because of security, and now she no longer feels secure there. It's not only the progressed Moon that indicates the need to change, but added to other things happening, it certainly speaks of her inner need to find a new home in the world.

Once your progressed Moon goes into the **11th house,** you are pulled to connect with your networks, with your work as it expresses your ideals in your community. The sign at the entrance to this house, tells you something about how you build your networks and interact with the ideals of your community, or your various communities. This is the time when you connect emotionally with the family of humanity. The contacts you make and deepen during this time have a special flavour for you. They have a personal meaning. The ebb and flow of feelings is strongest around any groups you belong to. Acceptance and rejection by groups is felt deeply. Reflecting on your personal life as lived in a community in this time opens you to reflection about every person and their lives lived in all the communities that have ever been since the beginning of our time and space.

And then your progressed Moon takes you into the **12th house**, via the sign on the cusp, which gives you information about the route into nowhere and everywhere. Your time here may draw you to hospitals and monasteries, if you live your 12th house literally. But it may also simply draw you inward, to a place behind the scenes of your outward, known life. Like the other two water houses, this is a house of secrets. But often, these secrets are hidden even from yourself. Recently, I asked a client who has a very active spiritual life what was happening. His progressed Moon had been in the 12th for a year or so, and he said, "It's odd, but nothing at all, really. I have always been most concerned with my soul life, and for the past year or so I find I can't be bothered. I guess I'm a bit lost there, but I don't feel unhappy. I don't know if this is a good thing or not."

He has his natal Moon in the 7th, square Jupiter conjunct Sun in the 9th. And he had finally found the woman who was to become his wife. It was as if the hunger that had always driven him was sated for a while. But also, his sense of his own soul had disappeared. We both thought it was fine, and that his soul was finding something deep enough to rest in. He said that he felt empty and full at the same time.

This is a mysterious house. I suppose it draws you to something less personal and more diffuse – your personal needs are met by everything, by nothing, by the ebb and flow of something beyond your conscious intervention. Let it drift there. Some part of your long history is being completed, and it is probably not appropriate to interfere too much. If there is more unhappiness than happiness during this time, then perhaps it can lead you to reflect on life as the Vale of Sorrow, which is really the Vale of Soul-making. There is deep mystery here, sacred knowledge, but not knowledge to be used by the ego-self.

And once it leaves the 12th for the 1st house, your feelings come awake again, and off you go on another round.

THE SATURN CYCLE AND THE LUNAR CYCLE

Audience: I keep thinking about Saturn, and the way it goes round the signs and houses in about the same time as the Moon. I know you said you will do that in the next seminar on the progressed Moon, but that could be months from now.

Audience: Or years.

Darby: True. Yes, the Saturn cycle is very much connected to the progressed Moon cycle. Let me say this for now. Get used to tracking your progressed Moon – attend it by giving it time. In other words, use your knowledge of where it is at any given moment and pay attention to the images and ideas that arise as you reflect. Notice the kinds of people that come into your life during each stage, and notice those to whom you have strong emotional reactions. Keep your eye on your emotional life, from the progressed Moon's position. You attend to it; it comes alive to attend to you. After a while you won't have to concentrate on it – it will be part of your imagination. It will return you to your past, and through that, connect you to the unfolding pattern of your emotional life. Not only to your human life lived here on this planet in this time and space, but also to all life in all times and spaces on this planet.

In watching transiting Saturn, you are seeing where the work lies at any time. The sign says something about a two-and-a-half-year period which everyone shares. It describes the, let's use this misused word, "energy" – the energy involved in giving shape to things. The house it is transiting tells you where you will have to work to give shape to things – the house where discipline and control and work bring things into balance and allow you to get some sort of reality around them. This is the area where a cold, dry eye is appropriate for your development, and where things might dry up for a time, so that you can work to bring them back into balance.

Now, where Saturn is drying up, the Moon is moistening things, bringing you into personal relationship with the issues of the sign and house concerned. Often this attracts you to people who can illuminate your connection to the things associated with the house concerned. We inhabit our structures with feelings. We live personal lives within the structures of society, and within the limitations and the security provided by these structures. Life demands that we work, internally and externally, with our limitations and our necessities. But life becomes dry and desiccated if we are not in touch with the feelings that connect us to our life source – with feelings that connect us to others, and to our past and our present. Ignore Saturn at your peril. Ignore the Moon at your peril. I mean the things that they symbolise – time-bound necessity, shape and form, limits and lessons and karma. Be aware of feelings, connectedness, the past, your body, your relationships, your soul and your power of reflection, which turns events into experiences into meaning. The two are inextricably bound together.

Audience: Onions must come under both Moon and Saturn.

Darby: Onions?

Audience: They are Saturnian in the sense that they are bitter, but they have all these layers which is the Moon.

Audience: And also they make you cry, which can be the Moon's response to Saturn.

Audience: Also, one gets to know one's onions. If you know your onions you are in good shape.

Audience: Onions are sweet.

Darby: Onions are sweet to some people and bitter to others.

Audience: Are onions good for you?

Darby: I don't know. But I do know lunacy has entered the room again.

Audience: Spanish onions haven't got any stamina.

Darby: Can someone open the door? Or a window? Or both? Does anyone have anything slightly more relevant to say before we return to our day-world?

Audience: Oh yes. I have got notes from America, where Steven Forrest lectured on the Progressed Moon, and he gave little anecdotes, little sentences. I don't know if anyone wants any...

Darby: Yes, tell us some of them.

Audience: The progressed Moon in the 2nd house. He says that when it first goes into the 2nd, you feel "a bit of an impostor." You feel like you are in a foreign country, without the ability to express yourself. You feel a lack of resources and confidence. You experience anxiety and insecurity about your lack of resources, and anxiety and feelings of vulnerability about control of money. After a while, though, that fades away.

Darby: That's interesting – the analogy of being in a foreign country and not being able to express yourself, because you don't have the resource. It's strange too, because I went to live in France for several months while my progressed Moon was in the 2nd. It's the strongest memory from those two and a half years. I have always remembered that time, in Libra in the 2nd, in terms of others experiences there. But, of course, there was the sense of anxiety around resources on all sorts of levels.

This is why I have only wanted to give you brief ideas and images to get you to connect with your own progressed Moon. The ideas I have expressed for each position come from *my* experience – my life, my clients and my friends. Our charts are all different, and we will each have another way of telling the story. The thing I really want to say today is: don't miss the opportunity the progressed Moon offers you, as astrologers, to deepen your experience of life through using the fertile Moon.

When your progressed Moon goes into any house, it is like that. It goes in and it is new, and you don't actually know how to behave in terms of that feeding ground. Then as it moves towards the middle of the house you become really good at it. You really run that Moon and that particular experience well. And as it fades away through the last part of the house, you actually lose interest in it somewhat, get a bit bored and are ready to let go of it in some way. It is the same with the signs. As you enter a new sign, you are really awkward in that sign, wearing those colours. I said I had my progressed Moon in Pisces. I am not really a pastel person at all. But with the progressed Moon in Pisces, that is what I am and that's very comfortable. Then, as it tails off, you are ready for a new wardrobe, so to speak. That's lovely. Another one from Steven Forrest?

Audience: Yes. Sure. Give me a number.

Audience: 1st house.

Audience: He says the 1st house is where a new tone is struck. It can be a new career. It is also setting the tone for the whole of the next thirty years, and it is finding out suddenly who you are and responding to it. He uses the phrase, "wise whimsy." And says, "Be whimsical when your Moon is in the 1st house, and it will pay off."

Darby: Oh I like that.

Audience: Follow your whimsies and the money will be in the bank later. "To thine own self be true," he says.

Darby: This sounds like Joseph Campbell's "Follow your bliss."

Audience: What's that?

Audience: He said that if you follow what really comes from your heart, then you cannot go wrong in the end.

Audience: You might end up poor, though.

Audience: Oh yes, you might end up poor and alone. But if you are really following what he calls your bliss, you will be happier than being rich and secure but having done something all your life that you did not love.

Darby: Yes, he is saying those who have the courage or the recklessness to follow their bliss get life on their side. And I think that is great for progressed Moon in the 1st house. You get a clear reflection of what really keeps your feelings alive.

Audience: Did somebody say they wanted the 3rd house? Progressed Moon in the 3rd house: He says it is "information hunger." The heart is curious and restless. It is exploring the environment and bumping accidentally into information. It is confusion, but there is a fleshing out and acceleration of the pace of life.

Audience: What about the 8th house.

Audience: The 8th house is disease, death and sexuality.

Audience: Oh no!

Audience: He was actually very fascinating about this. He says that the personal stuff is held distant, and personal stuff that has been held at a distance, when the progressed Moon comes to the 8th, all comes flooding back. Past loves that have been lost – there is a remembering of that. He says that when love goes bad, that is as bad as we feel.

Audience: My progressed Moon is in the 8th, from the natal Moon in the 3rd, and recently I went to a sort of school reunion and met a guy I'd been in love with when I was about twelve, and we started seeing each other. It is really weird!

Darby: Interesting. I think there is a purgation too – things are stirred up and purged through the intensity of feeling. It's the Scorpio story, but in this case it comes through relationship with other people. They "start" it.

Audience: He says it is life we have forgotten, but that is then remembered. Then, when it goes into the 9th, we are washed clean, as we are in all fire signs.

Darby: And the 12th?

Audience: He told an anecdote of two old people in a hospital bed. Both are dying. "A" has lead a colourful life, and he has followed his divine plan as much as possible. Whereas "B" has followed the more material American dream. He has made sound investments, watched TV and lost weight.

Darby: This was an American conference?

Audience: That's right. "A" has enjoyed life and "B" hasn't, and "A" is ready to die and "B" is dying angry. He was saying something about attitude to death and ending, to letting go.

Darby: And that is my signal to let go of this seminar. I hope you have got something interesting to work and to play with – something from which you can launch your own investigation. Next time we will look at the Moon in relation to the Sun – at its waxing and waning. This time we looked at its ebb and its flow. When everything is flowing in your life you can feel the abundance of life. When you are high and dry and feeling isolated from the flow, that is the time to reflect, to turn to that place of reflection which is there inside you. The habit of turning to it, of reflecting, always from a new vantage point, leads you naturally towards engaging with life itself more deeply, more fully – to engaging with this life in time and matter against the background of infinity, eternity. I am just reminding you of things you already know. And we have been putting these things we already know into an astrological framework.

Ok, let's stop and go out into the sunlight.

PART II

The Moon and Its Cycles

The Phases of the Moon, Athanasius Kircher, 1646

This seminar was given on 12 November, 1994 at Regents College, London, as part of the Winter Term of the seminar programme of the Centre for Psychological Astrology.

INTRODUCTION

Today we are going to consider the astrological Moon. First we shall explore the Moon in relationship to the Sun. We'll look at it through its cycle in the sky as it moves from the conjunction with the Sun to the waxing square, to the opposition, to the waning square and through the three days of darkness back to the conjunction. I'm going to use Dane Rudhyar's book, *The Lunation Cycles*, as the basis for our observation. I want to do this to honour his work and introduce it to those of you who do not know it. Also, I want to draw on his transpersonal vision, because it adds a dimension to modern astrology that is profoundly enriching. It widens the eye.

Then we are going to look at the progressed Moon in relation to the natal Moon – from birth as it moves on, by progression, until the outgoing square at around seven years old, then onward to fourteen, twenty-one and then the lunar return, at twenty-seven and a half years. And, if you are going to reach a venerable age, you will live through the whole cycle again. Now, as we know, this cycle pretty much coincides with the transiting Saturn cycle, which is twenty-nine and a half years. And so we'll spend a bit of time looking at the interaction between them in the natal chart. We'll end the day by tracking the two cycles through the chart of someone who has been kind enough to reframe the events of her life using the warp and woof of these two life themes. The Moon and Saturn not only represent the principles of opposites in the astrological story of life, but they are also profoundly tied to each other by the fact that their cycles coincide. Although interlocking, the two cycles are very different. We shall try to separate the threads today so we can see them more clearly.

CHAPTER 7

Sun-Moon Relationships

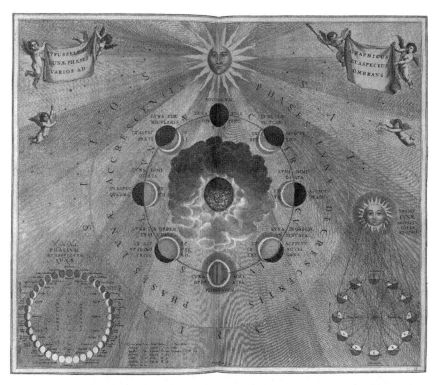

Lunar phases, Harmonia Macrocosmica, Andreas Cellarius, 1660

L et's first look at the Sun and the Moon in the sky. One of the great hardships of living in a city is that one loses contact with the incredibly beautiful dance between these two luminaries. Those of you who have lived in the country all your lives cannot imagine the night without the ever-waxing and waning Moon. Most people who live in the city cannot help but be less aware of it – except for those of us who are astrologers. And whenever we spend more than a month in the country, it is one of the major features of our life there. It becomes so alive to us.

From day to day, week to week and month to month, the Sun is moving around our zodiac in the sky, against the background of the constellations. We see it moving all the time, particularly at sunset and sunrise. Every day it rises and sets a little further east or west, depending on the season. It is always moving. Every night the Moon changes – you see it happening from night to night and you feel it in nature around you and in your own nature. Those few days before the full Moon, as it gets closer and closer – you feel the tension and excitement as it builds! And those last nights as it gets smaller and smaller and then disappears – don't you feel the touch of sadness that goes with it? Then there is the quiet of the dark of the Moon. Too quiet, unless you are waiting for it because you have something specific to do that can only be done in the deepest dark. But that is another story!

And then the slow return – sliver by sliver as it begins to grow again. Always the same cycle – completely familiar, and yet always different, because the Sun is ever moving on from sign to sign. So each New Moon, Full Moon, and all in between are different. To those who are sensitive to the skies, every Full Moon is different – they even look different. And of course, nature is different all the time, going from cold to warm to hot to cool and to cold again. And every month, though the lunar faces change in the same way, each face is a different face because they repeat it against the ever-changing configurations of the planets through which they move as they do their stately dance in the sky.

And isn't it interesting that although this is a dance between the two luminaries of our sky, we almost never see them together? We see the Sun in the day and the Moon in her phases through the night. We see the Moon changing her face, reflecting more or less of the Sun's light as the month goes on. The light is always the Sun. The reflection of the light is always the Moon. And the reflection of the light is a constantly changing mirror. The one time it is possible to see them together is when they are in exact opposition and you are on a wide enough horizon to see the Sun go down and the Moon come up simultaneously. We used to wait for that moment any time we were in the bush, in Africa, at the full Moon. And what about the magic of those days when the Moon is visible, high in the blue sky? Do you remember as children, seeing it and wondering how this could be? The queen of the night, pale and loitering in the daytime sky!

For us here in the West, the received wisdom of those things represented by the Sun and the Moon are heavily coloured by our culture's deep suspicion of everything natural, repeating, cyclical, instinctive, dark – what we now call unconscious; the realm given to the feminine. Those things represented by the Sun are coloured by our idealisation of clarity, purpose, linear development, light, spiritual development, and what we call consciousness: the realm given to the masculine.

Have you got any words, images, that particularly stand out for you when you think of the Sun and the Moon astrologically?

Audience: Sun is destiny. As you said, consciousness. The Self, in Jungian terms.

Audience: The masculine principle. The archetype of the father. Authority.

Audience: Creative self. The part of you that shines. The spirit.

Darby: And the Moon?

Audience: The feminine principle. Mother. Rhythms of daily life.

Audience: Anima, for men. Soul life, or the reflector of soul processes, as you talked about in the last seminar on the Moon. Emotional life, rhythms of feelings between yourself and others.

Darby: Yes. Actually, that thing about the Sun being associated with consciousness and the Moon being associated with the unconscious is a bit odd. Sometimes people's Sun is unconscious isn't it? They don't really know where they are going. They have no sense of destiny, direction, purpose. But they know what they are doing from day to day, and they know what makes them feel good and bad. So one has to clearly understand what people mean by these words, conscious and unconscious when they are used in relation to the Sun and the Moon.

In the late 1960s in America, we were taught, as budding astrologers, that the Sun was the thing you were supposed to aim for. You were here, on Earth, to achieve consciousness, and that was represented by the Sun. The Moon represented that which you were supposed to go away from; it represented the unconscious, and the task was to move from unconsciousness to consciousness. The Sun was the symbol for your spirit and your future while the Moon was the symbol for your past, your emotional attachment to your past. And it was taken for granted that you must move away from your past and towards your future.

Of course, the Moon also represented the habits of your daily domestic life. The Sun was also your father, and the Moon was your mother, but I don't remember discussing the implication of those connections. My memory might be faulty here. I don't have many notes left from that time. I was studying astrology in New England at the time, and it may have been taught differently elsewhere, or I may be misremembering. But I know we were supposed to head to the Sun!

Of course, this was all part of a philosohical legacy that takes us back at least two thousand years, and probably a few thousand years before that. We know that, in Neolithic times, there was a long series of clashes between cultures which were more lunar, nature-oriented, cyclical – feminine, we might say – and cultures which were more solar, aggressive, linear, monotheistic – masculine, we might say. The clash goes on today, doesn't it? In all sorts of ways.

The legacy we receive from our Judeo-Christian culture is pretty one-sided, at least in its teachings and writings – the solar principles of unity, integration, the constant striving towards an ideal of goodness, following external authority unquestioningly, and the rejection of inconstancy, instinct, feelings.

The Sun is the symbol that represents destiny in the chart – that spirit which animates you to shine your light The sign and house it is in describes where you reach for the stars. The Sun is our very own star – middle-aged, medium sized star, but our very own. And so it represents that which you reach for.

And how else do you reach for it, but through your day-to-day living? The habits and rhythms of your daily life, as expressed by your Moon, are the vehicle with which you get to your star, the Sun. You cannot find your way to the goal of your spirit, as represented by your Sun, except through the constant inconstancy of daily life. If the Sun represents your personal connection to the greater Spirit of the universe, then the Moon represents your emotional connection to the life you live from day to day in the light of the Sun – in the light of the Spirit of the universe. The Moon reflects the Sun in its Moon-like way; your day-to-day activities reflect your spiritual aims, your spiritual aspirations, your spiritual connection to life. The way you live your life; the way you reflect your experiences and find meaning in them, in turn reflects your relationship to existence itself. This is one way of saying how they are related astrologically.

As astrologers who look at the chart to get psychological understanding of ourselves and others, we take note of the Sun with its aspects and the Moon with its aspects as telling us something about what we take on from our fathers and mothers. We look at other things for this too – the 4th house, the 10th house, and their conditions. When there are aspects between the Sun and Moon, we think about the relationship of our parents, and how that affects us in our relation to others and to our lives.

We look at the archetypal father and mother in the Sun and Moon, and observe how they relate to each other. The Sun can be seen as the father ideal that you are seeking in your own human father. He may or may not live up to this in your eyes, but it underlines all your interactions with him. The Sun can also be seen as that ideal which you seek in those men to whom you give authority. The Sun is also your own point of authority, that which calls you to follow it because that is the only way to gain life's treasure – to be fulfilled, to have those moments when you are full of vitality, power and light.

And the Moon is the mother your soul is seeking, and often feeling, through your own mother. The Moon is that which you seek and often feel from women with whom you have emotional ties, the ebb and flow of emotional contact that you draw out from your sexual partner. The Moon is your personal well, pool, pond, lake from which you draw nourishment for your day-to-day living. The Moon is reflector – reflecting the light of the Sun in changing constancy to the waters of the earth. The Moon mirrors the Sun's light in its waxing and waning way, in the waters of our body. The Moon reflects the light of the spirit to the soul of our body – Sun to Earth's water, spirit to *Anima Mundi*. Our Sun is our spirit, mirrored in the waters of our own souls – our spiritual goal-direction mirrored in the rhythms of our daily contact with ourselves and with others.

So, how do we see this in our own lives through our charts? My first impulse is to start with Aries Sun, but...

Audience: We always start with Aries. Can't you begin somewhere else?

Audience: It's natural to start with Aries!

Audience: Spoken like an Aries!

Audience: But it's true too.

Darby: OK, let's start with Pisces. So you take Pisces Sun, and you think of how it might describe the father of one with Sun in Pisces. Perhaps he is experienced as not being there so much. He is a disappearing father or he is elusive in some way.

Audience: He is weak, or dissolute.

Audience: Or kindly, but ineffective.

Audience: Or he is saintly.

Darby: Yes. The Sun gives you your archetypal stamp for masculine creative energy. So, if your Sun is in Pisces then the goal-direction of your spirit is to express the characteristics of Pisces. Your father naturally carries that archetypal masculine, and you register him in a Piscean way. You pick up from him everything you can that is self-sacrificial, subtle, removed, soulful, lost, confused, dissolute, disillusioned, fishy, compassionate – any combination of those things, depending on the aspects to the Sun.

If you are a male child, then you will take these characteristics into yourself. If a female child, then you will tend first to give these characteristics away. I mean that you will tend to see them as outside yourself, particularly the negative ones. You will see them more in the men around you – look for them there. It seems to me women of our culture tend to take back these projections later in life – sometime in their mid- to late forties they begin to see themselves in terms of their Sun sign and aspects. Or perhaps I should say, they begin to live truer to their Suns.

So let us say that you are a Pisces male. From the very beginning, you have absorbed the Piscean characteristics of your father, taking in everything that fits that shape inside you. But you have done this through your mother, since it is her body that still holds and sustains you. In the very early days of your life, your father is absorbed through your relationship with your mother. She sets the rhythms – or rather they are set between you, and described by the Moon and its position and aspects. The Sun is shining out there, but it is too bright for your infant eyes. You are kept in the deep inner light of the Moon. It is only when you are strong enough to bear the day that you are brought out into it. Do you know that in many tribal cultures, the infant is not brought out of the home at all for the first three months?

Now, that Pisces Sun has to be lived out somehow on this earth, and the way it is lived out is through your Moon. So as a Pisces, you will be a dissolver. That is one of the words that might describe the image at the centre of your heart. You either dissolve because you are drunk all the time, or you dissolve because you are seeking some kind of spiritual oneness with life, or you dissolve people because you are so confused that every time you come near people they get confused. So your role is somehow to untie knots, to loosen knots in one way or another – either by stepping in them and confusing them, like a cat does with a ball of yarn, or because you actually step in to loosen where the struggle is, where the pain is, as a healer. But how you do that from day to day, from rhythm to rhythm, in relationship with other people and with the Earth, depends on your Moon.

If you are a Pisces with Moon in Virgo, you do this by fixing things and people. You are going to go around trying to make it right. If you are a Pisces with Moon in a fire sign, you are going to do it through some kind of wildness or inspiration – most unstable usually, but very exciting when it works. But no matter what combination you have, if you are a Pisces, you are going to be aimed at the dissolving of things, the breaking down of things. Wherever there are knots or tightnesses, you tap in. Wherever there are points of stuckness or rigidity, you tap in. And in dissolving, you are trying to dissolve yourself, dissolve your own ego-identity, because the more it dissolves the more you are serving the purpose within which you were born.

Audience: You can't serve the purpose of your Sun if you dissolve things destructively by being drunk all the time or chaotic.

Darby: So say we of the middle classes! I don't know. I'm not sure I understand enough about the mystery of the universe to say who is doing God's work and who isn't. Can any of us really say? What I do know is that the Sun and Moon can never be separated. The Moon reflects the light of the Sun to us on Earth. Your emotional life reflects the light of your highest aspirations in your day-to-day activities. Your daily habits reflect the light of your spiritual fire to your soul life.

To achieve your purpose, to let your Sun shine, to fulfill your destiny, you have to do it through the Moon. The Moon describes how you interact with life from day to day. It is this day-to-day activity and the daily rhythm of your own emotional and physical life that provide the ground with which you achieve your destiny. The Sun describes the images at our heart's core, and like sunflowers we turn to it. But it is the inner rhythms of our body and psyche on which we ride towards our Sun. In looking at the Sun, its position and aspects, we can see images of the goal of our spirits, and the forces, the factors, that will be the "rod and the staff" which drive us there. But we must look to the Moon to see how this destiny will be felt in the waters of the person – what kind of relationship life will attend this "destiny."

Audience: I have Sun in the 10th in Capricorn but I have Moon conjunct Neptune in the 7th, and I keep thinking that this Moon-Neptune gets in the way of me achieving my Sun in the 10th.

Darby: It's the idea that it gets in the way that gets in the way. The dreaming or wandering or wasting time is at least half the equation of achieving your own destiny. So to arrive at your own destiny, you have to go through your Moon. Pythagoras and his school were concerned with a lot of ritual. A lot of the ritual had to do with death and dying and the way to die, to get back to the stars. To get back to the stars, you had to go through the Moon. The Sun is simply the star closest to us, our very own star. To express our Sun, we can only go through the Moon.

THE LUNATION CYCLE

Phases of the Moon from waxing to waning

Now let's look at the relationship of the Moon to the Sun, using Dane Rudhyar's *The Lunation Cycle*. He calls it the soli-lunar relationship. This is a book that many of you have read, others of you know about, and perhaps some of you have not even heard about. Are there any of you who don't know Rudhyar's work? I see a few of you don't.

The Lunation Cycle came out in 1971. It had been published under a different title a few years earlier, and had originally been written in the early 1940s, but it wasn't until the early 1970s that it became widely known. I was in Africa and read it sometime in 1972 or 1973. In those days, astrology books didn't get to South Africa as easily as they do now, nor was astrology around much down there. I remember reading it, becoming very inspired, but being frustrated that there was no one to talk about it with. It is a beautiful conception and it informed my thinking, as did much of his thought, not only for me but for my generation of astrologers. I still think he is worth reading today. He is not always easy to read, but he inspires one to think and to experiment oneself, and that is probably the best thing an author can do.

Some time in March or April, the Sun and Moon are conjunct in Aries. The Moon moves away from that position in the sky, day by day, until seven days later it is in Cancer and square to the Sun in Aries. It waxes in light until 14 days later it is in Libra and opposite to the Sun in Aries. Then the light begins to wane, until twenty-one days later it is in its waning square in Capricorn to the Sun in Aries. The light continues to wane until the Moon, from our Earth point of view, seems to disappear from the sky and the night is dark. Of course, the Moon is still in the sky, but for us, it has gone. And then it reaches the position of the Sun again, but this time in a new sign, Taurus.

You can watch this process in the sky, if you are lucky enough to have a sky to watch, or you can track it in your inner sky, using the ephemeris. It is an ongoing process and it never stops, ever-repeating, ever-changing, always the same. At some point in this cycle, at some point in the year, you are born. And your birth will coincide with the Sun and the Moon being in a particular relationship to each other.

Rudhyar says that when the Sun and Moon come together at conjunction, a "seed idea" is incarnated. This seed idea may be understood as an image or a concept that expresses something of the sign in which the conjunction takes place. Presumably the seed idea of each sign will be modified and defined by, not only where the ruler of that sign is, but also its aspects and position. The Sun goes through each sign every year, but every year is a different time. And different times call for different versions of the twelve basic archetypes which are released year after year on this particular planet.

Now, he says that this seed, like any other, carries within it the archetype of the fully grown organism, and also the power to become it, once it is activated, he says, by solar heat and moisture. And he goes on to say that it is the Moon, moving through its phases in relation to the Sun, which brings that seed to Earth, so to speak. You could say the Moon incarnates the seed idea. He speaks of the first half of the cycle as the growing of the idea in the earth until it reaches fullness – in the full Moon – where it can be realized completely. In the first half of the cycle, structures are being built which will take the "idea." As the Moon wanes, that which has been illuminated at the full Moon is now slowly disseminated and there is a release of the creative meaning behind the original seed. This release is personal as well as transpersonal.

The Moon is servant both to the Sun and to the Earth. She is mediator, between spirit and matter. She reflects spirit to matter – she brings spirit into matter. She illuminates matter so that it may be receptive to spirit. She is the *Anima Mundi*, the Soul of the World. And in your chart, she reflects your *Anima Mundi* – the soul in your world. And this soul is reflected in your relationship life.

And so the celestial dance goes on and on, and at some moment in the cycle each of us was born. Each of us carries the imprint of that moment from our first breath. Rudhyar is very keen on checking out the New Moon before your birth. You can then get an image or a concept – sounds like the wave-particle duality, doesn't it? – in any case, a clue about the "seed idea" by looking at the chart of the conjunction. It is important to do this if you are to understand what he is illustrating. For many of us, the sign of the conjunction – the new Moon – will be in a sign different to our own Sun sign. And so for those of us for whom this is true, we must return to that earlier sign to imagine what might have been seeded, before our birth.

And this reminds me – before I go on I must tell you that I have brought his work into my own, and therefore much of what I say today will be mine and not his. I shall try to always tell you when I am quoting him directly, but much of what I say will not be found in his book. His ideas seeded mine. He got me thinking about this. I hope to get you thinking about it too, so that you can find a way to integrate it into your astrology. And of course that means you will change it too.

Audience: What you just said about the New Moon being in a different sign to your Sun sign – that is true for me. I have Moon in Capricorn, opposite Sun in Cancer. It is just past the opposition. But the Sun was in Gemini at the new Moon before my birth. Does that mean I would look at that Gemini conjunction to see the "seed idea" which is expressed at my full Moon birth?

Darby: Yes that is what I have been doing, as it seems the logical thing. You are a Cancerian, and so the spiritual goal-direction of your life has to do with the development of nurturing. And you do this in a Capricornian way.

Audience: Yes, through my business, with which I take care of my family and the families of my employees.

Darby: But the relationships you make, through which you reveal the impulse of the Sun, come from that new Moon in Gemini. The seed idea of communication of ideas is that which is revealed through your interactions with life. Through this you become a nurturer.

Audience: My business has to do with communication, and that I ascribe to my Mercury in Gemini.

Darby: And this is another dimension of that. In this dimension you are playing out the seed idea of Gemini, through being a Cancerian. Rudhyar does not say much about this side of it, but I have spent some time, over the years, in understanding and adapting his vision to my own experience. To get meaning from the soli-lunar cycle you must go back to the Sun-Moon conjunction before your birth. If it is in the same sign, well and good. Easy to understand. If it is in the previous sign, you must put a bit more thought into understanding it.

Now, you were born at a moment in this cycle and so you are the entity that will express the "seed idea" of the Sun in its sign, and you will express it through the Moon. The angular distance between the Sun and the Moon will tell you what part you play in the expressing of the seed idea.

As astrologers, we usually only notice their relationship when they are at certain key angles – the conjunction, the square (we rarely distinguish between outgoing or ingoing square), the opposition. Some of us have strong feelings about the quincunx. I have a friend who has a sesquiquadrate between Sun and Moon, and she is very aware of that. What Rudhyar did was to make us notice that they are always in relationship, and he gave us his images and ideas about various points in the cycle of relationship.

During my early years as an astrologer, in South Africa, before I got to know lots of people and got so busy, I followed the Moon and the Sun as they did their yearly dance. I watched them in the sky and I watched them in the ephemeris, month after month for a couple of years. It is a good thing to do, if you are becoming an astrologer. You begin to sense the changes that they are mirroring to us here on Earth. You see them move through the signs, and the houses of your own chart, touching off various aspects as they go along. Each New Moon becomes something with which you engage. You are part of the cycle, but you also become a witness to the cycle.

Rudhyar says that a seed idea is implanted at every new Moon. Remember, he is a poet and a visionary, and he describes what he intuits in this way. He says a "something" is seeded when the Moon conjoins the Sun in each new sign. The Moon picks up the seed idea, gets the message of it, in his manner of speaking, becomes the receiver, and as it goes through each sign it touches everyone, through their personal planetary configurations. The Moon disseminates the message of the seed idea as it goes through its cycle

You can feel deeper into the seed idea by seeing where the ruler of the Sun is in one year as opposed to another year. For example, on the 3rd of November, the Moon conjoined the Sun in Scorpio around 1 p.m., here in London. So the seed idea would have had something to do with elimination of the outworn. That is simply Scorpio. This purging of that which is no longer vital, and which, if not eliminated might contaminate the next stage of development – Sagittarius – can be further identified by Pluto in Scorpio, and by

Mars, which is in Leo now. As long as Pluto is in Scorpio, we are in a collective purgation, and where that is relevant to you is determined by the house it is in. Mars in Leo, as personal ruler of Scorpio, will tell you where, by house, a cleansing of any ego impurities is being pushed for.

Now, the seeds of this idea of elimination and purification were set off at New Moon, and for the next twenty-eight days the Moon separates from the Sun in Scorpio, waxing in light until it reaches full, on the 18th of this month. We are on the 12th today, and the Moon is in waxing trine to the Sun. If you look at where the new Moon took place, the house it was in, you see the place where this seed idea of purgation and transformation was set off for you.

If you follow the Moon through its waxing, through the houses of your chart and see where it is now, in mid-Pisces you can see how this idea has been progressing through your daily life. Anyone born today will be born after the crisis of the first quarter phase, but still quite a way from the full Moon. They will express, one way or another, the characteristics of this phase in their relationship to life. Now, as it moves towards the full Moon, where it will express itself in all its glory, structures are being built which will give form to the seed idea born at the earlier Sun-Moon conjunction in Scorpio. Once you are attuned to this cycle, you will begin to hear this particular symphony.

Remember, he is expressing something that he intuits – he knows that this cycle has meaning, and he uses the ancient symbology to translate it into concepts that have meaning for him. Don't get hung up on whether his translation is "right" or "wrong." Listen to what he is hearing, and see if you can hear something too. Then find your own way of expressing it. Learn to pay attention to the endless repeating, always new dance that goes on. The Sun, Moon and planets are there to *liberate your imagination*, not to enslave you with thoughts of what is going to happen next and next and next. Listening to them attunes you to the great in the small – the ever-repeating always the same, always different, cycles in life.

Every month throughout the year, the Sun and Moon conjunct in a sign and house, and go through the whole cycle of unfolding, illumination, disseminating and return, and go on to the next sign and house. If you are born with Sun and Moon conjunct, you are born at that moment of seed. If you are born with the Moon in waxing square you are born at the moment of crisis and turning. If you are born at the full Moon, you are born at the moment of illumination. If you are born at the waning square, you are born at the moment of disseminating. If you are born at the dark of the Moon, you are born at the moment of seeding. And if you are born at the conjunction, you are born at the moment of release of seed.

Let me put these up on the board so you can copy them down now.

The new Moon is from 0° to 45° away from the Sun.
The crescent Moon is from 45° to 90°.
The first quarter is 90° to 135°.
The gibbous Moon is from 135° to 180°.
The full Moon is from 180° to 225°.
The disseminating Moon is from 225° to 270°.
The last quarter Moon is from 270° to 315°.
And finally the balsamic Moon is from 315° to 360°.

You'll notice there is a sign and a half for each one – about three and a half days for each phrase.

NEW MOON

The New Moon takes in a sign and a half after the conjunction of Sun and Moon. So if your Sun is 0° Cancer and your Moon is up to 14° Leo then you are still considered a new Moon type of person. The Moon can be up to 45° separating from the Sun. This is up to about three and a half days after the brand new Moon. Now, Rudhyar says that new Moon people are impulsive, subjective and emotional in their responses to life and to people, to relationships and to social processes. The images he uses convey the idea that these people throw themselves at life, and are less interested in people for what they are than for what they stand for, what they symbolise. He depicts them as youthful in the energy they express in impressing their vision on others and on the world.

My experience of new Moon types is that they are often frail in childhood, but gain strength as they go along. They either have high energy, or none. They really don't understand when other people don't believe as they do, see as they do. Things are obvious to them, or not. Having both the Sun and Moon so close to each other, especially when they are in the same sign, it is as if they have no place to go, other than where they are. So either they are being nourished by the direction they are going in, or, when that direction is obscured, they cannot go to another part of their lives for rest and recuperation.

All or nothing. They have to consciously learn to take rest, nourishment – it is not natural. Spirit and soul are engaged in whatever is in front of them. Or it is not! If you are unhappy, you are thoroughly unhappy. If you are happy, you are thoroughly happy, because you are caught in that seed thing. And whether you are right or wrong you believe in what it is that you are doing. That is the only thing that you could possibly be doing. So if you are confused and lost, you are completely confused and lost. Sun and Moon conjunct people are only what they are at that time, and there is nothing else, so they can come across as very dogmatic – though if you see them tomorrow, they might be in a different position, particularly if they are mutable.

When the Moon is so close to the Sun, it cannot reflect the Sun, because it is too close. The further it gets away from the Sun, the more power it has to reflect. For this type, tracking the progressed Moon is particularly helpful, because as it goes round, you get a chance to find this other place from which to reflect your own life, your purpose, your direction, your spiritual connection with life.

In terms of parental images, it is said that the parents are seen to have the same values when the Sun and Moon are conjunct. You will pick up similar values from both of them, and this is probably true if they are so close to each other that they share the same house and aspects. You will get the same message from both of them about what is important in life. In relationship life there is a sort of "Take me (and my message) as I am or don't take me at all!" feeling about these people. And also a "Why don't you see things the way I do?" kind of innocence.

When the Moon's light is still so young, only a sliver in the sky, its light has a certain expectancy to it. We begin to see the light grow and we respond, emotionally, with growing expectation. Everything is in the future – the full light is still far ahead, but inevitable. People born in these first three days are so close to the light that they cannot always see things in any other light but their own. That is why they are called subjective. They travel hopefully, carrying their precious seed idea to a distant destination, untarnished by the experiences of a long journey – still dwelling in the light of the original images of the journey. They are hardly separate from their own spiritual task. They must be it with all their heart and souls. They experience their parents as spiritually one. Their parents are fused, or only separated, by a whisper, in the deep inner places where soul mediates spirit into matter and time. Now, the further away the Moon moves from the

Sun, the more likelihood there is of different aspects to each luminary. This can confuse our perception of the new Moon type. And of course, it is further disguised when the Moon has moved into the next sign from the Sun.

Audience: What about that?

Darby: The enthusiasm, the sense of newness, pioneering, is still there, and the lack of reflective power, the subjectivity, but the sense of clear message sent out by both parents is confused. Your relationship with each of them is very different, psychologically, and that can disguise the intensity of their mutual identification with the seed idea. In identifying one parent in a particular way and the other in another way, you can lose your clarity at times. But clarity returns as you connect with the source of your enthusiasm when it is brought out of daily events. Your new Moonness is still home base for the interplay of spirit and soul in this lifetime.

Audience: My brother is a Pisces with Moon in Aries. It is such a confusing combination. He is so selfish in his unselfishness. He is truly compassionate, but so angry about it all. It must always be somewhat confusing when the two are so close but in different signs.

Audience: My husband has Sun in Scorpio and Moon in Sagittarius in the 8th house. He is a demolition man. Nothing excites him more than tearing down an old building to make way for something new. He has a keen sense of beauty, so when he has to tear down a beautiful building for something like a car park, he gets horribly depressed, but he can't help getting excited at the same time. He says you have to clear the past to make way for the future.

Darby: Lucky you are American. He'd have a hard time here. But let's go on.

CRESCENT TYPE

This is the name for those who are born with their Moons from 45° up to 90° waxing from the Sun. The word crescent comes from the Latin word "to grow." This degree area starts with the waxing semi-square, and includes the sextile and the square.

Audience: What if your Moon is exactly 45° away from the Sun, or 90°? How do you know which type you are?

Darby: I suppose we could cut it down finely and say up to 44° and 59°, it is New and after that Crescent. I have to say I don't know what to do about that. Like most cusp questions, one must just muddle along. Feel your way – blend the two. It's hard if you need tight boundaries to feel safe, or if you believe in astrology literally. Cusps and confusing house systems are there to keep us safe from a world that might look like it could make perfect sense.

Audience: Perhaps I could explore cuspal people and make up a whole new system for those on the edge.

Darby: Oh yes, you could become an explorer of fractals on cusps – seeking patterns deeper and deeper into the edges which are offered by the cusps. Rudhyar says, about the Crescent type, that the impulse for action challenges the old. He says that it does this, "in a more or less intense struggle." This must depend on whether it is closer to the semi-square or the square. Presumably the sextile is the less intense struggle. He speaks of self-assertion, and faith in oneself. There is a sense of a command that has to be carried out, and one does it with eagerness. He says you can feel overwhelmed by the momentum of the past, and there is a need to "repolarise one's capacity for personal or social relationship." Otherwise the weight of "karma" pulls you backwards. He also talks about the shock of discovering the objective world.

So it is as if you are having to push forward, and do so eagerly, but with a powerful sense of the past not far behind. People in this phase do seem to have to push towards making relationships more conscious than is sometimes comfortable for them. It is as if there is an assumption that they should be able to relate without thinking about it, and everything will be alright. But their lives demand that they pay more attention, cultivate new ways of relating, be more conscious than is comfortable. They are carrying a spiritual impulse, defined by the Sun, into manifestation. And since this is done largely through relating, the manner of relating has to be attended to so that the message can be conveyed.

Audience: I am a late degree Gemini with Moon in late Leo. I think I understand what you are talking about. My instinct is to just tell people what to do all the time – I get so impatient with them. I always seem to be modifying this tendency – and there are other reasons in the chart for that – but from this point of view, it would be because I am basically a communicator and I won't be able to get through to people if I come across too bossy. It is something like that?

Darby: Yes I think you've got it precisely.

Audience: Also, from the parental point of view, my mother was definitely the dominant force in our home – our father was in the background. I am wondering now if his values were being megaphoned through her, maybe without either of them knowing it. He always seemed to support her. I thought it was weakness – a desire not to get involved in the upheavals – but maybe it was because she was laying down the law according to his true ideas.

Darby: You say "our home." Do you have brothers and sisters?

Audience: Yes, one of each. And neither of them have Leo Moon or Gemini Sun. They agree my mother was dominating, but it slid off them in a way it didn't slide off me. I must ask them how they saw their parental relationship.

Darby: Yes, because they will have different spiritual ideas – different Suns – and different roles in conveying these ideas, depending on where their Moons fall in the cycle.

Audience: You use the word "idea" – is that because you are a Gemini?

Darby: I'm using the word "idea" in the Platonic sense, well perhaps in the Christian Neoplatonic sense: the Idea in the mind of God. I could use the word archetype. Perhaps I like the word "idea" because I am a Gemini! Oh, and that reminds me, Marsilio Ficino, the 15th century Christian Neoplatonic astrologer, had Sun around 4° of Scorpio and Moon 12° of Capricorn. There is a sextile between them. He certainly speaks out of this type of Sun-Moon relationship. He was challenging the Church and his times, not only with his blending of astrology and Catholicism – he was a celibate Catholic priest as well as an astrologer – but he was also responsible for coining the phrase "Platonic love".

Ficino was a passionate man who had passionate relationships with men. He was also a celibate. He wrote to a friend of his that their relationship could be called Platonic love, because the love between them sprang from their mutual love of Plato, and did not include carnality. He certainly repolarised his capacity for personal and social relationships. And he gave us a new term for certain kinds of love, a love which is born of our mutual love of something else, and sometimes, someone else. Though the term "Platonic love" has been desacralised in our unsacred times, and usually means simply "no sex here." The new Moon Ficino was coming from had been in Libra. The "seed idea" was from Libra – which is all about bringing grace to relationships anyway.

FIRST QUARTER MOON

The first quarter Moon is from 90° up to 135° after the Sun – the waxing square, trine and the sesquiquadrate. Rudhyar says this represents a phase of crisis in action.

These soli-lunar phases are all about relationship. The Moon, of course, is always about relationship, to oneself, others and life. We could say that the Sun represents your life – life force, life direction, potency. As the Moon moves away from the Sun, it is reaching out to connect with life, emotionally, so it can live its day-to-day life in response to the call of its Sun, its spirit. By the time it hits the square there is a crisis.

Rudhyar says that the crisis is expressed in action, because you are seeking to build a framework which may serve "for the future objectification of a new social ideal and of a sense of interpersonal relationships." He says it indicates a strong will and an excitement, or as he puts it, "self-exaltation when faced with crumbling old structure." He speaks of a ruthlessness to consolidate new ideals.

And yet, these people are often caught between the past and the future. However, Rudhyar says they exhibit excitement when in emotional contact with the old, crumbling, falling down, the degenerate – whether it be art forms or institutions or a marriage. Whatever it may be actually galvanises you into action in some way, because that is a call to put something new into shape. And yet sometimes the

Sun and Moon in square to each other like this can create a confusion of values which makes it very difficult to act.

Audience: Someone showed me Timothy Leary's chart yesterday. He has Sun late Libra and Moon in late Aquarius conjunct Uranus in Pisces. I'd say he is certainly living out this relationship between Sun and Moon.

Darby: With every moment of his life, it seems, and at any cost. His was a very powerful voice for the 1960s people – he literally preached a new way of relating to each other and to our society, and he certainly exhibited a gleeful delight in the face of what he saw as crumbling institutions and social values. Since then, he has mostly been banned from media coverage, and he's been thrown in jail in almost every country he has travelled through, but it hasn't stopped him for a minute as far as I know.

Whether he is a destructive or constructive influence depends on your point of view – probably both, like most powerful people with vision. He is a very powerful example of this type of soli-lunar relationship. And he's paid a high price to be it, in his relationship life and in his natural human need for ordinary security. And yet, because there is a trine between the two, perhaps it doesn't feel as costly to him as it looks from the outside.

Let's look at a chart where I think it must feel pretty costly in emotional as well as material terms. We'll take a bit of time over it.

Audience: Is that the Queen?

Darby: Yes. Queen Elizabeth. The Royal family is easy prey for all of us, aren't they, because everything they do gets such publicity nowadays. I looked at this and I thought, "Well, she must be very excited now!" She is certainly faced with a crumbling institution. Isn't it wonderful that she is having such a wonderful time, because everything is just crumbling around her! But, to be serious, I cannot imagine that she is really enjoying it. Look where her Moon is, in relation to her Sun. It's in the 7th house of marriage. She has got the Moon there, and Neptune is there square Saturn and opposition Mars. You all know her chart already, don't you?

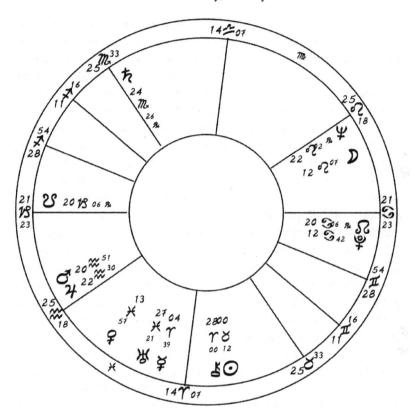

Queen Elizabeth II
21 April 1926, 1:40 am GMT, London (51N34, 0W10), Koch cusps

She is a Taurus with Venus in Pisces in the 2nd house, which further emphasises the idea of her Sun. Now, the "seed idea" that came in at the new Moon previous to her birth was in Aries, which is the original seed idea of each year. So the first impulse of that year, which leaps into life and unfolds throughout the year through all the other new Moons is that which she is building a container for.

Mars, ruler of Aries, was in Aquarius conjunct Jupiter, which was part of her Mars-Saturn-Neptune T-square. So the seed idea was going to have a rough ride into time and matter, pushed and pulled by the forces symbolised by Saturn and Neptune. She is a very public instrument of that rough ride.

She was thrust into a modern world, presumably against her Taurean nature, which would naturally have been more comfortable with keeping the established order going, year after year, pretty much the same. She was forced to partake in the modern disintegration and levelling process that is Aquarius. She must have a somewhat sentimental feeling about her own property, some of which, at least, she has had to open to the public. But letting go of things is part of Pisces anyway. And so it furthers her own spiritual development, even if it hurts. She has been having a hard time with that lately, hasn't she? How do you maintain and hold (Taurus), and give away (Pisces) at the same time? If you have got Venus in Pisces, you have to give away that which you love to get the love you need. So the impulse that gets lit at the new Moon comes to birth in conflict – public, private, her personal marriage, her marriage to her people, and her children's public disasters in marriage.

She was born just after the first square, but her Moon is in the 7th house. I don't know what happened when she was young, but when she married, she was faced with the fact that she would have to build on something that was crumbling – perhaps it was marriage itself. Right from the early days of her marriage, it must have been tricky, and she maintained and held herself in proper Leo-Moon dignity, or rigidity, for those of you who judge her uprightness as negative.

The interesting bit is that when it comes to the square, Rudhyar says, "In the face of crumbling structures, one seeks to forge something new." Is she trying to forge a new relationship with her people? With her husband? She would be doing it in a queenly Leo way. Perhaps she had to face her marriage crumbling – or her pride – and she sought to forge a new relationship again and again. She still seeks to forge new relationships with her public, although she also works to maintain the status quo pretty strongly. And now she is faced with all the crumbling marriages of her children. Will she forge new relationships with her children out of that? She also has Neptune in the 7th house as well, square to Saturn, opposition Mars and Jupiter.

Audience: Her father died soon after she was married.

Darby: When did he die?

Audience: 1952.

Audience: She married in 1947, and the King, her father, died in 1952. What happened in 1953?

Audience: The Coronation.

Darby: That's it. So the main thing about that first square is that it is crisis. Now, we know Sun square Moon is a "hard" aspect and therefore demands conscious attention. We also know that it indicates a conflicted relationship between the parents – or shall we say, the parental relationship is felt most strongly in its awkward moments. The tension between the parents is more noticeable than the ease. Her mother is the Queen Mother – a Leo lady if there ever was one. Our Queen has Moon in Leo in the 7th square Sun in Taurus in the 4th. She is known to have adored her father, and perhaps she noticed her mother's larger personality, greater ease and enjoyment of the public role, and the tension it may have produced between her parents. She was attuned to her father's solid, reliable, steady, quiet qualities, and to her mother's queenly, people-responsive, outgoing tendencies. She is presumably more like her father.

When the square between the Sun and Moon is waxing square, then the tension felt is the tension of the mother moving away from the father. The Queen Mother may have been working for the same end as her husband – bringing a sense of peace and stability to a disturbed people – but she was doing it in a Leo, 7th house way. The present Queen felt this tension and now must try to bring a sense of peace and stability in crisis after crisis, presumably in her own marriage, in her marriage with her public, and in her children's marriages – the consolidation of new ideas in the face of crumbling structures, crumbling stability. The seed idea is of stability in a crisis, and she is an instrument of the crisis and the struggle to build new social relationships.

So there is crisis, and she is a Taurus with Venus in Pisces, and therefore devoted to maintaining the dream or the illusion of stability. In that sense, she is a servant to love. But she is also a servant of the new Moon after which she is born. She is called to care for and be stable for that which she serves, and also to pioneer a new relationship with the people – Mars in Aquarius in that new Moon in Aries chart – with a lot of personal angst and frustration: the T-square. Even if she were not the Queen, she would have to hold onto and let go of everything that is hers – all her resources, which stem from her being – and become part of a new emerging order, in spite of herself.

Audience: What about a waxing trine between the Sun and Moon. When the struggle is not so great, or at least we might think that?

Darby: Nelson Mandela, for instance. Sun in Cancer trine Moon in Scorpio. He might be a good example of someone who works "for the future objectification of a new social ideal and of a sense of interpersonal relationships." He is a man with a strong will and an excitement, or "self-exaltation when faced with crumbling old structures" – a quiet man but one who has shown his dedication to the consolidation of new ideals.

It is fair to say that his life is about emotional contact with old, crumbling, falling down, degenerate structures! Because it is a waxing trine between the two luminaries, we imagine he does not have the personal sense of crisis in all the crises. He certainly does not look as tense as the Queen. His manner is more graceful. Probably there was not the tension set up in his beginnings through his parental relationship. The trine would tell us that.

GIBBOUS MOON

This type is born with the Moon from 135° up to 180° – from the waxing sesquiquadrate, quincunx and up to the opposition.

Now, I thought I would stay with the royal family for a bit here. The Queen's son, Prince Charles, follows neatly with the gibbous Moon. Dane Rudhyar says that as you move towards the full Moon you are working towards illumination. Prince Charles is born just before the full Moon, two days before. He is a Scorpio with Moon in Taurus, heading towards full Moon.

Rudhyar says that this type of Moon pays a lot of attention to their own capacity for personal development and personal growth. He describes them as people who want to contribute value and meaning to life, to their world. He says they are working to make some kind of revelation or illumination possible. They are likely to devote themselves to great personalities or to great causes, and they want others to work with them with the same devotion. Whatever we may think of Prince Charles personally, he certainly appears indeflagable in his work towards his chosen causes, and he struggles publicly with his search for illumination.

Audience: In-de-flagable? Don't you mean…

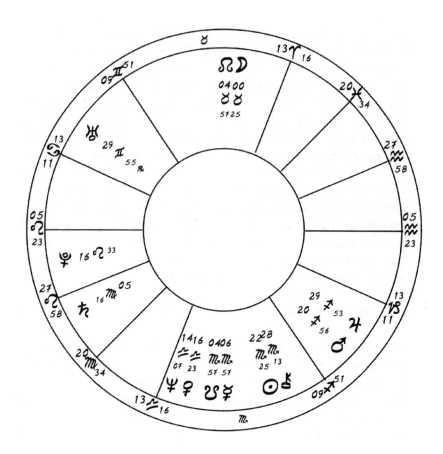

Prince Charles
14 November 1948, 9:14 pm GMT, London (51N34, 0W10), Koch cusps

Darby: No, I mean he never flags in his efforts.

Audience: I don't believe it.

Darby: What, the word, or the fact that he never flags? He is a Scorpio and born late enough in Scorpio so that the previous new Moon was in Scorpio. In Scorpio we see the death of all that is outworn – death and decay and purification – so that what is left are the bare bones, the essence of what was once released into life. The seed idea

in Scorpio has to do with the destruction of the old and the purification which will clear the ground for new life. In Scorpio we break
open and break up, so that a vision can be released in Sagittarius. This
is part of the natural life cycle – nature's way of making room for the
new. In Scorpio something has to break apart. A seed has to break
apart so that something new can be born. So, he is about something
to do with breakdown, but how does he do that? Well, he certainly seems to do it publicly. He has a position of responsibility (10th
house Moon) and we all watch him as he does his Scorpio destiny.
He does it being in a very public position. I can never quite accept the
general belief amongst astrologers which says that he won't be King.

Audience: That's because you don't want to believe it.

Darby: I have a terrible feeling you are right. No objectivity here.
Anyway, I choose to suspend judgement on it and just see what happens. He's got the Moon in the 10th and Leo rising. He's got Pluto
on the Ascendant square the Sun. He expresses his persona with
grace, but he also expresses a sense of danger in that he shows his
darkness, his capacity for depression and his attraction to danger.
And in his formalised world this seems to be self-destructive. But
he has to express it. Like all those with Pluto in Leo, he carries the
evolutionary urge to destroy and recreate himself. The ambivalence
of having power – the need for power or the need to break power
apart – struggles within him, and we see the struggle, the need to
break something. Look where his Pluto is, right on the Ascendant
in Leo. Something has to be destroyed so that it can be transformed
into something more appropriate for the times he lives in. He works
towards an illumination that will reveal what must be destroyed, not
only to himself, but to the public. And he does this through his position of responsibility, 10th house Moon in Taurus.

He carries this message of destruction and transformation
through his vocation, as Prince of the Realm. His Moon is in Taurus. The ruler of Taurus is Venus, which is in Libra in the 4th house,

conjunct Neptune. This tells us that he was born into a family where idealisation and disillusionment around love and partnership was played out in his early life – perhaps secretly, but he must have felt the whispers. It also tells us that his spiritual longings cannot be satisfied by the family, tribe, into which he was born – he is spiritually foreign to his clan. And he is searching for something that can perhaps be found in his old age.

Of course, it tells us much more than that too, and it will always be an aspect of mystery, not only to others but to himself. Perhaps it is part of his charisma, this deep, spiritual, sadness – this longing. Listen to what Dane Rudhyar says: "They ask repeatedly, 'Why?'; they work towards a clarification of personal or social-cultural issues, with some kind of, to them, important goal in view." They have a goal in view, and may not reach it personally, as they are part of a larger picture, just one moment in the evolving story. Their goal is the illumination, the full light which reveals the heart of the original seed. And with the ruler of his Moon configured so, it is probably also in response to a personal, early felt sense of confusion and loss, experienced through his mother's private disillusionment due to his father's elusive romantic behaviour. Do you see why I am saying this?

Audience: That Venus-Neptune in Libra in the 4th house.

Darby: Yes. I know several people with this gibbous Moon. Until I recently went over Rudhyar's work, I had fallen into the habit of seeing them simply as full Moon people. But I have begun to notice the difference between just before and just after full Moon now. In both cases, the message received from the parents seems to be opposite. These people do seem to be more objective about life than those born earlier in the cycle. They can have something happening to them and see it at the same time as "interesting." But in the waxing full Moon they are driven towards the light – towards reaching illumination, enlightenment, revelation. They are driven to achieve it personally because it seems important to life. In their childhoods they watch their mothers seeking understanding, illumination, in seeming opposition to their fathers.

Audience: What is the difference with the waning opposition?

Darby: I'll speak about that just now, but let me say something about the full Moon in general, first.

FULL MOON

The full Moon is the point of illumination. Rudhyar considers the new Moon and the full Moon the most significant moments in the cycle. This phase goes from 180° up to 225° away from its new Moon. Both are beginnings, but in opposite senses. The new Moon sends out the seed and the Full Moon reveals that which the seed was to become – the flower of the seed. Rudhyar waxes poetic about the full Moon.

I am using the chart of a country here, and one that is perhaps no longer relevant. This is the South Africa that I knew and the chart we used down there, and the one that we saw working. Transits and progressions spoke through this chart. I thought it was appropriate to use it because of what has happened in South Africa. This is a full Moon chart.

The Sun is in Gemini with full Moon in Sagittarius, but the seeding, the New Moon before this full Moon, took place in Taurus. Venus, ruler of Taurus, was in Aries. Its only significant aspect was a trine to Uranus in Leo. So the seed idea of deepening and grounding spirit into matter has a sense of urgency about it. When the full

Moon occurs two weeks later, the Sun has gone into Gemini, and South Africa was born just after the full Moon.

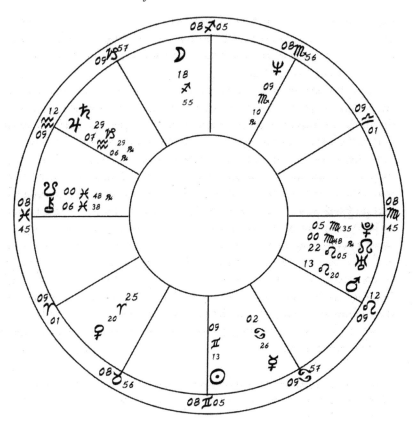

South Africa
31 May 1961, 12:00 am (22:00 GMT on 30 May)
Pretoria SA (28S45, 28E10), Koch cusps

Rudhyar says that the opposition is the apex of the cycle. The original impulse is now clearly seen – it is a clear image. He writes, "This may mean a revelation or illumination, and normally some kind of fulfilment; but it can also mean, negatively, separation or divorce – perhaps even a divorce from reality, or inner division..." He goes on to say that relationship is all-important to this type, or else he rejects all relationships except those with "an ideal or "absolute" character.

Objectivity of pure consciousness is the basis of character – revelation, illumination and fulfilment. "The negative is separation and divorce from reality." It is a very radical position. All of us have revelations, but one does not always move, change one's life through revelation. The white people of South Africa – signified by their leaders – generally shared in the revelation that they were the masters and they had the right to be served by the black population of South Africa. Individuals may have felt differently, but the country expressed this collective belief and was able to believe if for a very long time. And then, recently, as we have all seen, that revelation became outdated, seriously outdated. It became profoundly divorced from the reality of the times.

The tension built, until a new revelation took over, in the shape of two prime movers: F.W. de Klerk and Nelson Mandela. Mr. de Klerk has Sun in late Pisces and Moon in late Capricorn, so he is part of the last quarter Moon cycle, which we will address just now. He attended a dinner here at the end of May with Margaret Thatcher, John Major, and various businessmen. A friend of mine was there, and when she left she came to a dinner party I was attending. She told us that de Klerk was asked, "Why did you do it? Why did you actually do it? What policy were you moving from?" And he replied, "God told me. I had a revelation. I had a dream," or words to that effect. "God told me." My friend burst into tears, to her embarrassment. But more embarrassing, she said, was that there was a feeling in the room of, "Oh. Yes, interesting. Sorry we asked."

He is a Pisces with Neptune on the ascendant, if the chart we have is correct. And in this case, he was speaking, he was functioning, as the voice of that South African chart – of that South Africa.

Audience: And of the New South Africa. According to Nick Campion, who sets it for when the new constitution came into effect, it has Sun in Taurus opposite full Moon in Scorpio! So now, according to this way of seeing, there is a new revelation from which the country will be moving.

Darby: Yes, exactly. And this new chart is also an example of the new Moon having been seeded in the previous sign, because the Sun is about 5° or 6° Taurus and the Moon around 20° Scorpio. So Aries new Moon was the original impulse – not just the original impulse, but the original impulse of that particular zodiacal year.

"Relationship means everything to Sun opposition Moon people, or the repudiation of relationship." In the time of that chart there was a clear relationship between black and white. It proved to be discordant with the times. The relationship crumbled and now there is a new relationship developing. At the moment it is chaotic, but it is a new relationship based on a new revelation. And now we have a new chart.

"Relationship means everything or repudiation of relationship, except those with ideal and absolute character." In other words, there is a sense that there is a truth here with the opposition, and you follow that truth until you have a revelation that there is another truth, perhaps at some point in your life, and then you follow that truth. Anyone who doesn't follow that truth with you, you can not be in intimate relationship with, because you are burned by the illuminations that happen to you in your lifetime, and you move out of them, you move from them.

Individuals with this full Moon opposition reveal the seed impulse, set out at the new Moon, in their lives. They feel the pressure to express the seed idea at the core of their being through the activities of their daily lives. Their soul life is connected to revelation of this seed idea. They do this through the distortions of their personalities and characters, as revealed by their total charts. Sometimes their expression of this revelation is very destructive and sometimes very creative. It is said that the Buddha was born with Sun in Taurus and Moon, full, in Scorpio.

Audience: He died with Sun in Scorpio and full Moon in Taurus.

Darby: Yes, isn't that interesting? One would assume that meant that his work of revealing the seed idea of Taurus at that time was complete.

Do any of you know the work of Thomas Merton? He had full Moon in Leo, opposite his Aquarius Sun. The new Moon he was "seeded" from was the previous one in Capricorn. He was a monk in a contemplative order. By the end of his life he was known throughout the religious world as a man who was dedicated to the renewal of the contemplative life, and prayer, in the modern world. He was open to the insights of non-religious thinkers such as Heidegger and Albert Camus as well as the contemplatives of Zen Buddhism, Hinduism and Muslim Sufism.

You might say he was open to anyone who had looked into eternity, whether they had found God there or not. His life and daily work reflected the discipline and rigour of a monastic life. The seed he is manifesting is from Capricorn. But he was an Aquarian, and he brought as many different kinds of mind to his task to updating an ancient tradition as he possibly could. He died in 1968 at the age of fifty-three. One day I shall do a seminar on a theme where I can show you his chart, in light of the work he did to awaken the modern heart to the extraordinary light at the centre of existence.

Audience: My husband has Sun in Gemini and full Moon in Sagittarius. He is part of the process of bringing satellite TV to this country. He believes in it absolutely. In fact I have never known him to do anything that he does not believe in absolutely. I call him Mr. Mission. The only time I ever saw him depressed – and it wasn't for long – was when he had to work for a period of time for something he did not believe in. He got ill with it all. But then he got out and he said he'd never make that mistake again. He has Venus in Cancer and they'd offered him enough money to buy the home of his dreams, but in the end he said it was not worth it, and quit before he got the home. I was distressed at the time, but later I realized his life and vitality were actually more important to me than a dream house.

Darby: Had it been your dream too?

Audience: I thought it had for a while. It is sort of collective, isn't it? And I have Venus in Capricorn trine Neptune in Virgo. I have to say that I have not always been so supportive of his dreams. Some of them seem a bit far-fetched. I have a lot of earth in my chart! But that taught me.

Audience: What about the parental relationship of Sun-Moon opposition?

Darby: The parents will seem to be pulling in opposite directions with both the waxing and waning full Moon. Loyalty to one may feel like disloyalty to the other. There is hatred of compromise, yet the necessity of learning compromise. Those characteristics are evident in both sides of the opposition. But I have noticed a difference between the two, and you must make your own study on these things, as each of us adds to the body of knowledge all the time.

What I have noticed is that, with the waxing opposition the mother's seeming opposition is because she is striving towards her own spiritual revelation. She feels something out there that is pulling her away from her husband, at least at the time of this child's birth. She is reaching for something of meaning. She is not yet there. If she does get there, it will be some time later. The child grows up with a sense of expectation, which becomes part of its own relationship life, its soul life. With the waning opposition, she already knows that her values are different from those of her husband. She is simply living with that knowledge, and may or may not do something about that in the course of her life. The important thing is already known. It remains only to do something about it, or not.

DISSEMINATING MOON

This is the name Rudhyar gives to people who are born with the Moon between 135° and 90° before the new Moon again. It includes the waning sesquiquadrate, quincunx and the waning square.

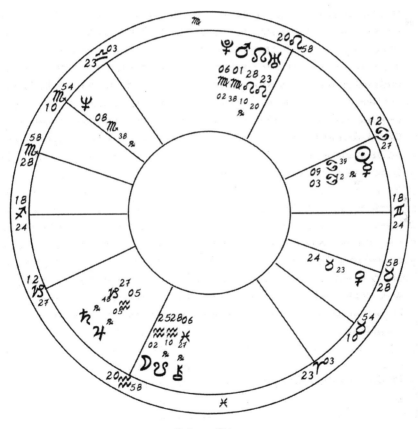

Princess Diana
1 July 1961, 7:45 pm BST, Sunderland, Norfolk, (54N55, 1W23), Koch cusps

Now we are truly heading home again, if home be the end of the cycle awaiting the next new Moon, the new seeding of the naturally following idea in the year. This is called the disseminating type. It is leaving the full Moon and going towards the square.

Here I am back with the Royal family again. This is, of course, Princess Diana's chart. She falls into this category. She has got Sun in Cancer in the 7th house, and Moon in Aquarius in the 3rd house, which is opposition Uranus and square Venus in Taurus in the 5th. Again, the seed impulse is set off at the new Moon in Gemini two weeks before. Mercury is in Cancer at that time so we can imagine that the Gemini seed of communication has a Cancerian undertone. She is so much a Cancerian, and everything she does communicates that message. It has to do with the communication of her nurturing capacity, but the way she expresses that message is through the Aquarius Moon, which is in opposition to Uranus and square to Venus.

The impulse for expressing her Cancerian spirit – for being a nurturer – is very strong. But she has to do it her T-square way. She has to do it through her own awkward, on-off rhythm. She has to respond in ways that other people find unpredictable and erratic. She can only take advice in short doses, and can only follow it if it catches her when she is in the right position. And mostly she has to do the opposite. Have you ever tried to give advice to a Moon opposite Uranus person?

Audience: Yes, my son. And it was not until he was seventeen that I finally learned that what he needed was a reasonably developed argument for the opposite of what I thought was best for him. That seemed to give him the freedom to follow what was best for him, at least according to his lights. I had to learn astrology to learn that.

Darby: Back to Princess Diana. She cannot hear what is being said, feel what is being said, unless it is completely disinterested – detached from self-interest. I wonder how often she comes across people who are truly disinterested, with her personality and in her position? That ancient Cancerian message, that archetype, of mother-nurturer, she can only do in the most modern and therefore most fragmented way. And her inner feeling must be that she can never get the kind of nourishment she needs from others, with that Moon square Venus.

Now, Rudhyar says of the disseminating type: These people demonstrate what they have learned. They are disseminators of ideas. They are popularisers of ideas. They are crusaders. He says, and I quote here, "...the negative type can easily be lost in a Cause and develop fanaticism or be swayed by mass emotions." I thought of everyone I knew within this group, and observed the crusaders at work. The revelation has happened and now there is work to be done. It is easier with the trine, of course, less resistance, but it is still there. The disseminating type is not as clear about what the revelation is, but it leaps to the feelings of spreading the message. There is again a tension, especially in the square, because one is so far away from the original seed idea, and one is heading back towards the Sun, which will incarnate a new idea.

Audience: My wife is a Pisces with Moon in Scorpio. She is a disseminator, and it is so natural that it doesn't feel like crusading, but when I think of it this way I see that she is. She has Sun in the 11th house and Moon in the 7th and she works in the area of development of communication in organisations. She is very successful at breaking through blocks in communication that happen in the organisations that hire her. She says her work is to melt barriers between people who work in groups together. She is very clever and not easily swayed by group emotions, because she is so focused on discovering the block and using the ideas she gathers – she reads everything relevant to her field – to melt their resistances to working together as a team.

Darby: She sounds like a good example of this part of the cycle.

Audience: She is, but when she wants to block someone out, she is frighteningly good at it!

Audience: That Moon in Scorpio. My husband has it in the 7th too. Great blockers!

Audience: Do you know Michael Jackson is a full Moon in Pisces? He has Sun at 5° Virgo, and so the new Moon would have been in Leo. And his Sun is conjunct Pluto, and his Moon is square Saturn.

Darby: I'm sorry we don't have time to look at that chart now. But it makes sense that the original impulse would have come out of Leo. And yet, he is a true Virgo, of his Pluto in Virgo evolutionary group. So from this, we see that the seed idea that you relate through with your Moon is sometimes different from your spiritual archetype, your Sun. I wonder if that is spiritually confusing? Let me go on.

To sum up: The illumination is behind you. Now it is about scattering the seeds that came from it. Full Moon people live the revelation, but now people born in this part of the cycle have to move to get it into the body of mankind. Their task is to begin the process of integrating what has been revealed, through their own relationship to others, to life. That is why they can seem like crusaders. They can feel as if they are in a race against time, with the Moon coming up to its final square before returning to conjoin the Sun.

Do you know that Albert Einstein was born in this part of the cycle? He had Sun in Pisces and Moon in Sagittarius, the approaching side of the waning square. His new Moon was in Pisces, and his Sun 23° Pisces. Think about not only his work, which reframed our notion of material reality in ways we have not even begun to fully understand, but also about the crusade which came out of it. He spent all of his adult life trying to stop the use of the bombs that were his brainchild – his brainchild, in the sense that they were built from the information he gave science about the construction of the atom. And, oddly enough, even though he was certainly probably one of the most lofty brains of our times, he is known to everyone in the Western world – not only his face, but what he did as well.

Do you see the underlying pattern that Rudhyar is responding to? You may find different ways of perceiving what he opened up, when you begin to explore it. What intrigues me is how he brings a vision of the yearly dance between the Sun and Moon down into the particular. Each of us is born at some point in the cycle and will naturally fulfill the part we have to play in that cycle. Whether we do it badly or well, willingly or not, consciously or not, is dependent on other things. But we are part of a natural cycle, and as the Soul of the World reflects the realm of Spirit in all its limitless but circumscribed way, so we are part of that. Our Moons mediate between eternity and time, between spirit and matter, imagination and realisation. And they do this according to nature's way as expressed by the celestial dance between our Moon and Sun.

LAST QUARTER MOON

Once you hit the last quarter, the square, you have another crisis point in the cycle. The last quarter is from the 90° square to the 45° semi-square. It includes the waning sextile. You get people here like Margaret Thatcher, Bill Clinton and Carl Jung. In the last quarter, Rudhyar says it is the time for the embodiment of ideological beliefs in definitive systems of thought or concrete institutions. People who are born during this phase force issues at all costs, in both personal and social relationships. They lack flexibility. They see themselves as pioneers who will only be appreciated later.

He says reformers belong to this group and they are geared to a future they only intuit. I thought this was a particularly interesting observation and that it was a good description of all the people I could think of born in this part of the cycle. Jung expressed his sorrow and disappointment at the end of his life that his work had not spread very far. He felt his whole life had been dedicated to work which was not really appreciated widely enough. He certainly lived a life dedicated to the embodiment of ideological beliefs in definitive systems of thought and in a concrete institution. However, that institution keeps breaking apart and reforming itself today in our Uranus-Neptune in Capricorn time.

Audience: Margaret Thatcher certainly fits the bill. I don't know enough about Clinton.

Darby: None of us do because he is still too young. These people seem to give themselves to something that will not be fully realized until they have left the field. Rudhyar says that these people generally have irony and humour which they put in service to their cause – or they are incapable of taking criticism at all. Perhaps both are true at the same time. I tend to think "both/and" is usually truer than "either/or" when we are talking about human beings.

As I am naturally attracted to people who have irony and humour in relationship to their own cause, I find that I have a lot of friends who were born in this phase. In these people I have noticed a recurring struggle with their sense of knowing something absolutely and having to let go of it for it to be realised. They know something, and they want to hold onto it, but if they hold onto it then they are not going to live in a way that might actually embody it. It is a big theme of that ingoing square. So the outgoing square is really struggling to build something, a new structure to contain the coming illumination, we might say, and the ingoing square is really struggling to let go of its feeling of possession of the revelation. Seeds can only grow in the dark.

Audience: I have that, and I struggle, struggle, struggle, but eventually give up and say, "OK, I give up, I can't do it." Once I have given it up, it seems to get a life of its own. It's just happened recently. I have the Sun in Virgo in the 9th square Moon in Gemini in the 7th. I have had terrible trouble with the person who lent me the money for my business – he was supposed to be a sort of silent partner but silent is the last thing he is. At the beginning of this year I decided to give it up – to just let it go – sell it and give him back the money. We had a confrontation. It was all decided. And then he fell in love and went off to live in Denmark and I got two big commissions in close succession and I was away! We finally seem to have reached solid ground, after trying for two years.

Darby: That's a very practical example of the expression of this phase. Thanks for that, Virgo! Does it speak in other ways?

Audience: I don't know. Yes I do. Every girlfriend I have ever had has had to handle me trying out my current beliefs about relationship. I am married now, and my wife bears the weight of my ideals about relationships. She is more down to earth than I am. I guess I get into trouble when I try to make the ideal real, but I have to do it. And then I have to give it up. I feel the force of it. I know I am right, but I know I have to give rightness up.

Darby: And the difficult thing must be that you cannot let go until you really do let go. With the dark of the Moon ahead, as a perhaps unconscious knowing, you have to fight to stay in the light of your own vision.

Audience: Yes – I tried getting philosophical before I feel it, but it doesn't work.

Darby: Jacob and the angel.

Audience: How?

Darby: I was thinking of something one of the sangomas said once – the tribal healers, the witchdoctors, that I worked with in Africa. She was telling me about the call of the spirit, and how you absolutely have to give in to it or you will die. But you also have to fight it for all you're worth. To give in before you are really beaten weakens you – or signifies to the Spirits that you are weak. To not give in at all kills you. To fight right to the end, and then to let go, takes you to the point of transformation – the blessing. Jacob fought with a demon all night, and in the morning he saw it was an angel who now wanted to get away from him. And he said to that angel, "I will not let you go until you bless me." And once blessed, he could climb his ladder to heaven.

BALSAMIC MOON

People who are born with their Moon less than 45° waning towards the Sun fall into this group. They are born up to three and a half days before the conjunction of Sun and Moon. Rudhyar again waxes poetic with this phase. He says people born in this phase are prophetic. They feel themselves to be the end product of a past and yet they are turned towards the future. They have a sense of destiny. He says they have a sense of their lives as a shrine or a "field" within which something is to be done, or is being done. Often they are willing to be sacrificed for this, their personal life being less important than whatever it is that can be done through them – to bring the past through to the future, to the new seed time.

This is the time when the whole cycle "comes to seed." It is the seed of the next part of the cycle – the idea of the next conjunction is born in the dark of its time. Relationships seem to be the "end of some process and the means of reaching some transcendent goal." Here I think Karl Marx was a good example. And in a more poetic vein, so is Bob Dylan, with his balsamic Moon in Taurus just behind his Sun in Gemini. I seem to know a lot of people at the moment who were born in this phase. They would not all say they are willing to be shrines! But there is a powerful sense in each of them, of the past as it is dying into the fires of the future. When the Moon conjuncts itself again it will be in a new sign. It is going to be a new impulse and a new seed, so there is a sense of expectation in them. But they are born at the very end of a cycle of life, and so there is a Piscean sense of weariness, of wanting to infold again.

Audience: A symbolic 12th house – you could go through the whole cycle with a book of the symbolic house positions it represents. Prince Charles is symbolically the 6th house, as it were. He is critical and discriminating. And that is supported by his Saturn in Virgo.

Darby: Yes; it is most satisfying when one dimension of the chart supports another, isn't it? But to return to our Balsamic Moon: here, the last traces of the original impulse, activated at the previous new Moon, are being carried. Those who are born into this moment of the cycle feel the weight of the whole of the story, as told through this cycle. They feel the weight of the past, but also the pull to give over their burden – to give it over, to fertilise the new kingdom. There is often a feeling of impersonality in these people. Relationships are chosen which will further the completion of an emotional process that often stretches back generations, but will also reflect the possibility of a living spiritual goal. There is a sense of urgency here, and relationships are based on the feeling that something important must be achieved, no matter what the personal cost. It can feel like a great burden.

I have a very close friend with this Moon, and he often speaks of the feeling that the past, history, weighs very heavily on him. He comes from a long line of public servants, in a rather grand way, and he feels the weight of this family's history of public service. He has not followed his family's tradition and yet is absolutely certain he has a task, and that this task has to do with something that must be resolved from the past so that the future can be freed. He plays this out in all sorts of ways in his day-to-day life. It is often very foggy, veiled, confused, but the sense of "something to be give over" is very great indeed. He has Mercury conjunct Neptune in the 9th house trine Uranus conjunct Mars in the 5th house, so you can see how one dimension of the chart supports the other.

And that reminds me: We are looking at different dimensions here. The soli-lunar cycle expresses one dimension, the natal chart another, the progressed chart another, midpoints another. We can uncover meaningful patterns in so many ways. Some of you will find that one dimension is more open to you than another. Some of you will find you can move with ease from one to the other, and see the reflection of one in another. It is very important to find out what works for you, and to be true to that. Most of us have to try various systems and methods; we have to explore as many ways of seeing as we can. But we all find, in the end, that some things speak more clearly to us than others.

To get familiar with this particular cycle, it is probably a good idea to watch it closely for a couple of years. You can begin at any new Moon, but it's worth paying close attention at the Aries new Moon, which is the beginning of the cycle, each year. Remember to note the position and condition of the ruler of the Sun, each New Moon. And then simply observe. Seven days later the Moon squares the Sun, and then fourteen days later it opposes the Sun and then seven days later it squares the Sun again, and then it returns to the

Sun, but in Taurus, because the Sun is now in Taurus. Then the soli-lunar cycle repeats its dance into Gemini, and then into Cancer, and so on through the year. Through observing it closely, with your body, mind, feelings and imagination, it becomes part of your perceptions. You begin to see that the relationship between your Sun and Moon is just a moment in that cycle. You are part of something much bigger. You have a part to play in this greater play. You are one of the dancers, but the dance has gone on long before you entered it and it will continue long after you leave. You are a participant in a sacred dance between Sun, Moon and Earth.

Watching this cycle is one of the ways of getting more in relationship to life itself, rather than always being caught up with whether we are getting what we want from this or that moment in life. Attending the cycle itself is one way of attending the unfoldment of life on this planet. Of course, this unfolding is continually happening through you. You can watch it as it moves through your chart. Each new Moon happens in the succeeding houses of your chart, and so you can see the cycle as it works its way through your life too. Sometimes the new Moon happens on one of your planets, and you can imagine the "seeding" as it touches your own life. You begin to see the seed idea, with its message, unfolding through time. Feel it in the waters, the earth, the air and the fire of your self. Follow this cycle for a period of time and feel the rhythms between the two luminaries, until this dimension of the dance of the heavens becomes part of your inner knowledge of the beauty in our sacred art.

The Moon, reflecting the Sun's light to Earth in its characteristic way, tells us the story of the individual soul as it goes about its day-to-day activity. We all do our daily round of activities, but each one of us has an image that illuminates our hearts, no matter how deeply we may lose track of it at times. Each of us plays a role in time. That role in time reflects the light of that which is, to us, eternal.

CHAPTER 8

Progressed Moon to Natal Moon

Now we are going to look at the progressed Moon cycle – the Moon as it moves, by progression, away from its natal place, around the chart, forming aspects to the natal Moon, until it returns to its own place, around the age of twenty-eight. On the way around the chart, it will, of course, touch every planet in the chart. It will move through every house. And once it returns to its own place it will start out again and go round again. And, if you have the strength and fortune to achieve old age, then it will make that cycle one more time. So most of us will have two cycles and some part of the third, and some of us will have three and maybe even part of a fourth cycle of the progressed Moon in our lives.

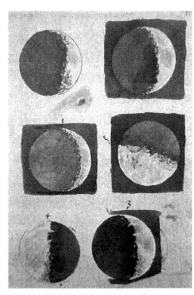

Phases of the Moon, Wash drawings by Galileao Galilei, from Siderius Nuncius, The Starry Messenger, Italy, 1610

Let's begin by refreshing our memories. The natal Moon describes the physical gateway through which each of us must enter if we are to have a life on this planet. So far, no one has discovered another way to get onto this very colourful little planet, circling its own medium-sized star. To spend any time here, as far as we know, you have to enter through a woman's body. And that woman's body will contain traces of every event that has happened since the very beginning of whatever it is that began. On another level, it will contain traces of every feeling that has ever been felt, since the beginning. All of the past will be contained in that body – some from the ancestral line of the woman who bears you into this life, and some carried into her with the sperm of the man, who impregnates her, and who is your natural father. But even beyond this, the body of your mother carries traces of everything, going back to the birth of the universe.

The past, as absorbed through your particular mother, will be channelled through the expression of the astrological sign your Moon was transiting when you were born. The sign will describe which of the twelve great archetypes will express and circumscribe all of these experiences. Your emotional nature, built on the emotional history of your ancestry, will be reinforced by the relationship that develops with your mother, once you are born. For astrologers, this will be further defined by the position and aspects of your Moon. All of the deep past carried by your Moon will be activated first with your physical mother. She will be the earthly source, from which you arise, and she will be the screen on which you project your feelings, until you become independent enough from her to begin projecting them onto someone else. This process of throwing our feelings onto each other and having them reflected back, distorted or otherwise, is one of the gateways through which we may find our way to truly relating to ourselves, others and life – though it may seem like a hall of mirrors for a very long time.

The Moon describes our instinctive responses, developed over lifetimes and gathered up out of our ancestry. They are absorbed through the soil in which we grow – our mothers, our source. Once we leave her body, they are brought out, activated, by the circumstances of our infancy. Those things reflected by the Moon get reinforced by our surroundings; for most of us these surroundings have our natural mothers at the centre. For some, this is not true. On the astrological level, however, the Moon that is in the sky, and therefore in our inner sky, is continually going round and setting off the lunar position and aspects again and again. Every day the position and aspects of the Moon are getting reinforced by external and internal circumstances. We are being deepened into life. And the astrological dimension reflects the physical dimension. The physical dimension reflects the astrological.

So, on the one hand, our history and the circumstances of our early nurturing into life are grown into habit patterns that return us, throughout life, to our source and therefore to our infant responses. But on the other hand, from the day of our birth we are moving away from this source. It is the progressed Moon which tells this part of the story. On this symbolic level, month by month, the progressed Moon is moving away, one degree by one degree, from its natal place. Life, as expressed by the cycle of the progressed Moon, is taking you away from your source, and towards other sources of life.

Each succeeding sign and house it enters symbolises new experiences and people. Each new experience brings up our instinctive pattern of responses, but each experience offers new life too. So there is a kind of paradox. The way you relate is "conditioned and unfree" – dependent on influences that are part of your unconscious life. And yet your way of relating is the only way to find your true relationship with life. On the one hand, your source experience is being reinforced continually, but at the same time you are separating from that source and moving towards an existence that includes other people.

Audience: And with other people there is always the possibility of love...

Audience: Or at least some sort of relationship.

Darby: And these experiences are archetypal and universal, and so also connect you with your common humanity, which returns you to a deeper source, which is partly in time and partly in eternity.

As the events of our life unfold, we are drawn forward. But this forward is not a straight line – it is circular, perhaps a spiral. It is a forward that always returns us to the past, as it carries us into the future. If you are willing, it can draw you deeper into that past, beyond your early conditioning, to a source deeper than memory.

The familiar feelings that arise at any turning point, any crisis, are the feelings that can take you beyond your own personal experience. These feelings that are psychologically attached to your mother, are the entrance to the deep waters that return you to the deepest source of your life. These feelings that arise from your ancestral past are the river on which you may travel to this source. This source is both temporal and eternal. Through developing the habit of reflecting on time and eternity, we reach, and are nourished by, the waters of life that flow beneath and through our own lives. This is our true soul food. It is the heart of everything we are seeking when we reach out for love, and it is hidden in every encounter, no matter how distorted the expression. The progressed Moon tells us the story of our emotional journey through life and it also shows us the entrances to the underground, underwater caves that open out to universal ground, universal waters. There are moments when the doors to these depths are naturally opened.

We will track the progressed Moon now, looking for some of those moments: when the present draws the past and the future together, when the present constellates the past in such a way that you liberate your future. Are you with me so far?

Audience: Liberate it forever?

Darby: No, not that. Not necessarily. The sort of liberation I'm speaking about here has to be won again and again. How often do we get into an emotional state which is completely familiar, in circumstances which are new? Because we are psychologically aware, we see in these circumstances the trace of the past that has set off the emotional pattern. But we are still lost in the pattern itself and cannot relate to the bits that are new in it – we are stuck relating to the bit that activated the emotions. I have been watching the progressed Moon since 1969, and I've noticed that at each angle – when it squares its own place, opposes its own place, squares it again, and returns to itself – these periods of time coincide with relationship experiences in which you turn a corner into new stages of inner development. It is more subtle than turning a corner – we can only talk in circles here! By attending these moments, you can keep moving into the unknown, where infinite possibility lies, rather than simply being unconsciously drawn to repeat the same pattern over and over.

Of course you will repeat the pattern – I don't mean to mislead you. The Moon is about repetition and constant return. But when these angles occur – progressed Moon to natal Moon – the coinciding circumstances and people are a gateway. At this gateway there is a return to the past through repetition of your deep emotional patterning, and at the same time the pull of the unknown, the new element in the situation which speaks of infinite possibility. If you attend carefully, you can allow your natural relating pattern to be taken into new territory, but you can also develop the habit of noticing new innuendoes and new layers of yourself and the world around you. Your Moon and its position and aspects are always reflecting your past conditioning. Every experience, if it has any emotional content at all, will constellate the same sort of problems. And yet, every emotional situation touches the chord that takes you down to your source, which can take you right through to the source of your being. In this way time and eternity intersect. We watch the Moon watching us.

Attending the past, through recognition of your own patterns of behaviour, while noting the new form that is presenting itself through the present circumstances and people, leads us into the unknown, where new forms of freedom and responsibility lie.

Sometimes we don't want to move into this unknown future. A client came to me on Friday. He comes to me every year for a look at the next twelve months. In the course of our conversation he said, "Another annual board meeting coming up – they are so boring, always exactly the same." Because I was thinking forward towards this seminar I said, "But that's not possible. The planets are always in new relationships to each other and you are always in a different relationship to yourself and to other people. Nothing is ever the same." He wasn't too interested in carrying on that line, so I had to drop it for then. He is a man who has decided what life is about, and he has settled into his role. And the thought that infinite possibility, the unexpected and the mysterious, are often hovering around the edges of the predictable and the known, does not intrigue him in any way.

Later I took it up with friends over dinner. We talked about how easy it is as we get older to notice the sameness of things and people rather than the differences, the newness – and, in fact, how most new things are greeted with great suspicion, the older we get. We thought about the planets which are always moving into different relationships with each other, and how their constant, changing, always repeating cycles reflect the same story in nature, and how in that, we are part of nature. There is endlessly repeating sameness within endlessly unfolding neverbeforeness.

It is in the second and third cycle of the progressed Moon that we get a chance to navigate the territory of our own emotional life and our soul life. After the lunar return, just before twenty-eight, the progressed Moon begins its journey again. But the other progressions have moved on, and the transiting planets are making new aspects all the time. During the first twenty-eight years, every movement of the progressed Moon coincides with the opening up of new territory for you. As it goes round the second time, it revisits every point again, and so through it you are returned to your past through the experiences of your present. But you are returned to the past through current emotional situations, and if you pay attention you can live the present all the way down to its roots, rather than simply repeating the same emotional pattern again and again.

Audience: Do you mean that the same sort of things happen again?

Darby: In a way, I do mean that. Let me use myself here, to explain what I mean. My progressed Moon is in Aries...

Audience: Ah, that's why you are willing to use yourself as an example.

Darby: Yes, I hesitated, but I can't resist! When my Moon entered Aries, at the beginning of this year, I went back in my ephemeris to see when it had been there before. I knew it was just under twenty-eight years ago, of course, but I wanted to see the exact period. I spent a couple of months returning to that time, remembering the sorts of trouble I got myself into in those years! And I remembered the quest I was on too, and the excitement and newness of things. I looked at the transits I'd been having during those two and a half years and reflected on the sorts of events that had coincided with them. Every once in a while I have an emotional encounter which sets off the memories of that earlier Aries Moon. My emotional reactions are very similar, but I certainly have more choice about my responses to those inner feelings this time.

I also looked at the previous angle of progressed Moon to natal Moon, which occurred about two years ago. I was at the incoming square, and am now on my way to the lunar return, still several years away. During the month of the lunar square I remember thinking that nothing significant seemed to be happening. But the lunar realm is so often hidden, and I knew something would emerge that would tell me a story. Now, looking from two years away, I can see one encounter during one evening of that month where the present flung me into the past with such a jolt. I remember the impact from here, but at the time was too busy experiencing it. The past rose up through the present. I sat and marvelled, but at the time I had no way of expressing it.

The experience felt universal, and yet the situation was very particular. I did say to someone, "I feel like I'm in a time warp." But I had to get a distance from it to see how much a part of a bigger story it was. It was a story that began at my lunar return and turned a dramatic corner at the first square. I've lost the connection at the opposition, but I was in psychotherapy at the time, and so it must have expressed itself in that deep space. This incident returned me to my lunar return story. But it is not complete. I keep wondering what will happen at my second lunar return. Will it be complete then?

Now that I am a third way through the sign, and a third way through the seven-year cycle leading towards my second lunar return, I stop here and there and notice this or that response to situations and return to the earlier time to remember myself. This is what I mean by bringing yourself, with your past, into the present. Each emotional relationship returns you to an earlier time, and gives you a chance to catch up to yourself. This reflection somehow has the power to free you to be just that bit more available to the present, and therefore the eternal dimension that underlies all experience in time.

If we can use the reflective power of our souls to attend that which is unchanging in the constantly changing, and that which is changing in the endlessly repeating, then we may develop the capacity to take nourishment from life, and to give it back, wherever we find ourselves.

Audience: That is asking a lot.

Darby: We may have less external freedom than we think, and also less internal freedom than we think. But if we have any at all, it resides in our hearts, and if our hearts don't make such choices, where is the possibility of any real freedom?

Audience: But most people, including myself, find the unchanging in their inability to change themselves or other people. I am watching my daughter as she keeps repeating the same pattern over and over in relationships. She falls in love with men who seem to be different but in the end hurt her the same way each time. I can see that she has learned this negative pattern from me. I couldn't change it and now she is repeating it. This is unchanging – how can she, or I, take nourishment from this?

Darby: I don't know how to answer such a question in the time and space of this seminar. I certainly can't say anything about your daughter, who is presumably young and getting to know her own nature through relationships. It is different for you, who are on the second round of the progressed Moon. Time and experience have given you scope for a deeper level of reflection.

I do know that those who attend to their inner and outer lives with care and reverence, navigating their desires, rather than being driven by them, do gain the ability to relate more directly to life as they go along. And I am certain they do it through deep familiarity with their native patterns, not by trying to escape them. The very pattern that causes you to repeat the same mistakes, is the pattern that is your gateway to the unchanging, from which all change arises. Through care and attention our perceptions are refined. Through contemplation, our reflections take us deeper into the nature of our life, which is life.

It is time to say something about the Saturn cycle. Because the transits of Saturn have roughly the same periodicity as the progressed Moon, they are inevitably linked to each other. In the first twenty-eight years they are very closely connected – the first progressed Moon square to its own place can coincides with the first Saturn square to its own place. The first lunar opposition will be close to the first Saturn opposition to its own place, as will the last square of each to itself. The variations in the time between them has a lot to do with how fast the Moon is moving within one section of the lunar cycle.

The lunar return and the Saturn return happen within two years of each other. But the older you get, the more the two cycles separate. This is because the lunar cycle is twenty-seven and a half years, and the Saturn cycle is twenty-nine and a half years. By the time of your second lunar return, they are separated by about five years. The lunar return happens first, and then four to five years later, there is the second Saturn return. And the third returns of the Moon and Saturn are separated by up to seven years.

This tells us that our emotional development (Moon) and our character development (Saturn) are closely linked in our early years. The development of our souls (Moon) and the development of our sense of responsibility to ourselves and to other members of our society (Saturn), are closely aligned in our youth and early adulthood. But the older we get, the more these two become separate things. The development of our relationship with life, through nature and through other people (Moon), slowly separates from our internal lawgiver (Saturn).

The rules and responsibilities we must confront and come to terms with during the first half of our lives are closely connected to our inner development, but in middle and old age it appears to be different. We still have to deal with rules and laws and limitations and boundaries, of course. Much of Saturn's realm has become embodied in the form of creaking bones and limitations on external energy. But these limitations, and the recognition of new stages of limitations, which imply new rituals and disciplines, and new responsibilities in terms of this recognition, no longer seem tied in the same way to the dimension represented by the progressed Moon.

Audience: Is this saying that the soul slowly gets free of time, the older we get?

Darby: I don't know, at this point in my life. But it is a most interesting comment, by the universe, and worth attending as we get older. Those of us who keep watching ourselves and others from the Lunar-Saturn polarity might have quite an interesting conversation about it, in about thirty years.

With Saturn's cycle we are dealing with the world of form. With the progressed Moon we are dealing with the world of content. Each stage of the Saturn cycle tells us about the structure of a life and the responsibility incurred by the nature and extent of that structure. Saturn tells us where the work lies and what kind of work will bring the possibility of mastery. The Moon tells us who it is that does this work. It gives us clues about the emotional nature of the inhabitant of this particular life. It gives us clues about the soul life of this inhabitant. And the progressed Moon tells us where the soul is taking nourishment from life. Saturn describes the shape of the life at any point and the progressed Moon describes who it is that inhabits this shape. I shall attend more to the lunar cycle, but the Saturn cycle will show its lines inevitably as we go along.

FIRST SQUARE: BUILDING A NEST

The square of your progressed Moon to your natal Moon occurs around six or seven years old. You have grown from infant to baby to child. It coincides with a phase during which you turn a corner in your emotional and social development. You are no longer an infant or a baby. You are not yet grown up, but you are feeling the pull towards independence very strongly, while still needing home.

Audience: And this is happening around the same time as the first Saturn square.

Audience: And the Uranus semi-sextile.

Darby: Yes, and that gives us the flavour of the freedom one begins to feel around this age, if other things don't interfere. Do you remember I said that these angles open us up to the possibility of new freedom and responsibility? We already know about the Saturn cycle following closely behind the progressed lunar cycle. But have you also noticed that the Uranus cycle is interwoven, at different sorts of angles, most of the time too? We'll keep an eye on it as we go along.

At this age, society begins to assume we can take a bit more freedom. We are no longer seen as babies. We are generally expected to have a sense of who we are in relation to other children. We often have an awareness of who our parents are in relation to other parents. We begin to have a conscious sense of who belongs to our tribe and who doesn't. We know to whom we belong, and we begin to know something about social hierarchies. The boundaries of our world, as inherited from our parents, begin to become clear. These things fall within Saturn's realm. They can be described by Saturn's transit. But there is another thing that is happening which is better understood in the light of the Moon.

The development reflected by the progressed Moon has to do with something internal and often very subtle. It is about movements in the inner life and has to do with the awareness of oneself as part of others, and yet also alone. In the womb, and in the first months and years of life, we are not really apart from eternity. We are nature, and respond from our natural urges. Day by day, month by month and year by year we enter time and space – we become aware of our separateness, our uniqueness. Inner and outer separate. As infants, we are one with the Soul of the World. We are animal, flower, fish – responding to inner urges in a rhythmical way. By seven or so, we have reached a stage where we are no longer "unconscious." We have grown to recognise the distinction between ourselves and others. We are cut off.

Audience: This sounds like Saturn.

Darby: Yes, this is reflected in the Saturn square. But the lunar square speaks of the need to merge with nature again. We find a secret part of ourselves, and we nourish ourselves there. We were merged, with our own needs, with our mother or family who supplied them, at least enough to keep alive. Now we begin to reflect on our lives in such a way that we find the need to build a place where eternity can reside. Around this age we have begun to reflect on life, our own life mostly, in such a way that we forge a relationship with life. Rather than just being life, we begin to have the power of reflection. And that reflection leads to the assumption of responsibility, Saturn, but also to the development of our souls.

Everything is building towards independence but still we need parental caring. Around this age there is a crisis, back to the past, forward to the future. It is reflected in our inner and outer life. And during this time, because we are moving away from our enclosed world, belonging becomes very important. We become aware of tribe. It is around this age, in America at least, that we start asking each other, "What are you?" and the answer is, "I'm French or Irish, German, Swedish," or "I'm Irish Catholic," or "I'm native American." And then, "What are *you*?" We were curious about each others' roots.

It is around seven that we become aware that people belong, not only to families, but to tribes. In some way you identify yourself in these terms, but you also long to belong to a tribe amongst your own peers. You belong somewhere, to a family or a group, or a person, but your inner self is seeking a new place of belonging. Some of us do not find that with other children, and there is a great sense of loneliness. Something is missing.

Audience: I was ill around that time and had to stay home from school for several months. I discovered books, and the people in my books became my other family.

Audience: Those questions about roots you were speaking about – America is a Cancerian country. That's why we all know where we all come from.

Audience: That's right. I seem to remember at that age, in a Capricorn country, it was, "Do your parents vote Labour or Conservative." Which meant, "Which class are you from?" That would tell you.

Darby: So early?

Audience: Yes.

Audience: "What does your father do?"

Darby: Yes, I think American children ask that too. And all of this is really finding out about tribes – discovering where one belongs and finding out where other people belong. If you are strongly Uranian you will, of course, be happier with people of other tribes. If you are Neptunian, you will seek the people who sing your song, no matter what their social tribe. And if Pluto interacts very strongly with your personal planets, you will probably feel alone amongst all the tribes, and seek to forge your soul deep outside the known places of habitation.

Audience: I didn't start school until I was nine. We were moving around too much. What I remember is that around seven or eight, I suddenly looked at my mother and thought, "You cannot be my mother. I must be adopted." But I was still afraid to oppose her.

Darby: Oh yes, that is interesting, and it stirs a memory. I think I have heard it before from people when they were talking about this time of life. And what it reminds me of is that transiting squares of planets to their own place always have this push-pull between the past and the future – fear of letting go of the past, the known, no matter how unpleasant, against the natural urge to grow into the future, the unknown.

This is the time during which a container is forming, within your own psyche. A part of you, which has emerged out of the "Eternal Now," builds this container to contain the part of you which longs to return to its eternal home, and yet is more and more lured by the things of time and space. During this period between the lunar square and the Saturn square, both the container and the contained are shaped. Having been cut off from the Soul of the World, you seek a home for the bit of it that is your own soul.

Audience: Which coincides with First Communion, in the Catholic Church.

Audience: What is First Communion?

Darby: It is when the Catholic Church first initiates the child into the Church. There is a period of preparation for taking First Communion – I think it was a year when I was young – and then you participate in a ritual where you are given Communion, in the form of bread and wine. From that moment you are part of the Church and are considered capable of making moral decisions. Before the actual ritual, you make your first confession – having reflected on your life so far and having remembered all of the sins you have committed so far – such as lying to your parents or teachers, committing acts of unkindness, and so on. It gets you into the idea of good and evil and gives you the responsibility for making moral choices. Before this ritual, you are not considered able to make such choices and so you are incapable of sin. After this, you are considered responsible, morally responsible.

Audience: So early? It's a bit young, isn't it?

Audience: I don't think a child would be expected to address the same level of moral complexity that an adult might be expected to. This is the beginning of one's moral life.

Audience: There is also that phrase from the Jesuits: "Give me a child 'till the age of seven and he is mine for life."

Audience: Scary. Do they really say that?

Darby: It is one of the things you hear floating around the Roman Catholic world. But the point is that it is around age seven where this initiation takes place, if you are born a Catholic. In other cultures there are other rituals that take place at this age, other coming-of-age rituals. I have never heard of any that take place earlier. Of course there are always rituals at birth, but it is around seven when rite-of-passage rituals usually first happen. The Roman Catholic Church is interesting because it still observes its ancient rituals and takes them very seriously. However, even if you were not part of a formalised, collective coming-of-age ritual, something of import is usually remembered from that time – something that signals you to the fact of your own existence, you own mortality.

Audience: I have Moon in Aquarius in the 6th house. The first square was in Taurus in the 9th house. When I was six or seven my nanny took me on her boyfriend's motor bike for the first time. It was enormously exciting. I felt so grown up. Also my best friend moved to another town and I missed him terribly for a while. But more to the point, a friend and I set up a church in the garage and I took the role of preacher and gave sermons to the neighbourhood kids.

Darby: Wonderful 9th house expression! Did they listen?

Audience: I'm a Gemini Sun in the 10th house. They listened! For a while, until we all got bored. But during that time, I decided I wanted to be a priest, but someone pointed out that girls couldn't become priests. I was really annoyed. After a while I got interested in something else – bricklaying, as a matter of fact.

Darby: Good Taurus stuff. Today you could more easily have gone on to become either a priest or a bricklayer. That's a fine example of this phase.

Audience: How is the second time around similar to the first?

Darby: Let me go through the first round here and then I'll say something about the second round. The first one is the basis for the other one or two you will experience, and so it is important to understand it.

FIRST OPPOSITION: FALLING IN LOVE

In pre-industrial societies this is another major point of initiation. It occurs between thirteen and fifteen years old. And again, the Saturn opposition will happen within a year or two. Uranus is around too, in the form of a sextile to its own place. The sexual development of people of this age is taken very seriously and rituals are enacted which will keep the tribe from blowing apart, with all that sexual energy on the loose. Puberty rites are enacted and marriages begin to take place. Our society also has its rituals, but they are less formalised. Or perhaps it is that they are not understood so clearly. And marriages only take place occasionally.

Yet, there is a dance going on. At this age children are no longer children. Our society no longer knows how to honour this time, between childhood and adulthood, and it has become a very troublesome time for many people. A lot of it has to do with the fact that we are educated for so long, sitting in chairs endlessly throughout our most chemically powerful years! Our hormones are racing around so fast our heads are spinning most of the time, while society tries to cool us down by packing information into our heads.

From Saturn's point of view, the opposition to itself, we come up against our society's rules and laws, "shoulds" and "oughts," in the form of parents and teachers and other authority figures. Many of us develop a rebellious attitude to all kinds of authority and tradition. Some of us get on very nicely during this time, but it is usually because we learn to hide from our elders and even sometimes from ourselves. The rest of us struggle with ourselves and the system. This is the time when you are most likely to hear mothers say, "I cannot even recognise my child."

That is the essence of the lunar opposition. At birth we were still fused with our mothers, sharing body and soul. By the age of seven, we have come some distance away from her, but we were still close to what she knew, from birth. We are beginning to find nourishment in our surroundings, in ourselves, from our own inner or outer tribes made up of those who share our interests.

By the age of fourteen or so, our need is to move as far away from her as we can get. At fourteen, we are seeking nourishment for our newly emerging selves. We are seeking to find our souls in others. We are longing to throw our soul out to be caught by someone who will reflect us back in such a way that we feel complete again. Our hormones are driving us out of our bodies and we are seeking to find a home in someone else.

Audience: At my lunar opposition I was sent away to school, due to family circumstances. My mother did not want this and neither did I, but necessity ruled. I have Moon in Capricorn in the 9th, opposition Uranus in Cancer, both squared Neptune. I was terribly unhappy for about two and a half years and then I made a friend and things got better.

Darby: In your case it was not your choice to separate. Yet it happened. It was time for you to separate, and you might have done it yourself, if fate, indicated by the outer planets to your Moon, had not intervened. When fate operates, it is hard to know what our real feelings are. They are caught up in the feeling of fatality. However, you remind me of something. This time is not only about sexual longing. It is the longing of the soul to find reflection in that which is other. It is the longing for communion with others – to find oneself reflected in another who is reflected back in the depths of oneself.

Everything feels so intense during these years. We are lost to ourselves because it is the time to find ourselves outside of ourselves. We dream. We imagine that we will be recognised by another who will return us to ourselves. We look for ourselves in everyone around us, and through our relationships we discover ourselves. We fall in love. We fall out of love. We get hurt and disappointed, we betray and are betrayed by others. We are driven to communion and our deep emotional patterns are played out with each other.

Perhaps this is the first time, in the natural order of things, that we have a chance to see ourselves as others see us. Over the seven years of this phase, we discover things about ourselves that delight us and we discover things about ourselves that hurt us. Through our intense emotional experiences, we are shaped and reshaped until some of us lose our shape, in trying to please others. And some of us withdraw into ourselves because we cannot find another who will reflect our inner selves back to us. We hide ourselves away, so that others cannot hurt us, cannot find us. It is often a time where art and music become truly alive for us.

Audience: Yes, that is what happened to me in the lonely time before I made a friend. I took up both painting and the flute, and I have never put them down, except briefly at the birth of each of my children.

Darby: You actually took them up for life. I think that is unusual. Most people reach out to music by simply listening to it a lot during this time. Both art and music express the soul, individually and collectively, and we begin to really feel the reflection of our inner selves in the images and the harmonies and disharmonies that we are drawn to. We find our own reflections in the true creations of artists.

Audience: I shudder to think what my son finds in the music he listens to.

Darby: And if I remember correctly, our parents shuddered when they discovered the books and the music we were listening to in our teens. During the first few years of this phase, we often seem as unlike ourselves, to our mothers, to our families, as we can possibly be. Emotionally, we are as far from our infant beginnings as we can get, as far from confluence with our mothers as we can get. For some, this is a satisfying experience.

Remember, the mother is also fourteen or so years away from the birth of this child too. Her progressed Moon is opposite where it was at this child's birth. Mothers who have kept up with their own inner development can enjoy the different relationship that opens up during this time. The two new perspectives can reflect each other with delight. I know several mothers for whom this is true. But often, in our society, there is a struggle between the mother, the parents, and the child.

Recently I did a tape for a friend in South Africa whose child has just turned fourteen. She was frantic because her child was disobeying her for the first time, in a major way. They are part of a very close family and consequently it showed up all the more starkly. Her son has a Libra Moon so you can imagine. He was a charming, accommodating and graceful child. But his Moon has progressed into Aries now. His natal Moon is in the 2nd house, so now there he is in the 8th house and he has gone all silent and sulky and he won't cut his hair properly and he won't dress neatly any more. He is definitely not graceful in his behaviour anymore.

Audience: And she is frightened. I can sympathise with her completely. My son has Moon in Virgo in the 2nd house and when he was fifteen his progressed Moon was in Pisces in the 8th. I couldn't believe what happened to his room! And the friends he brought home looked as though they had been sleeping on the streets all of their lives. He's a Capricorn with Sun in the 6th, and once when I asked him – I admit I was in a rage – who these people were, he snapped at me, "They're my research! I'm finding out about life outside your antiseptic, tidy walls, do you mind?" I did mind. And we raged on at each other for a few years. It was awful. His father just retreated into his work – I was the one engaged in full battle regalia. My Moon is in Aries and so I really went wild.

Darby: Where are you at now with each other?

Audience: Well, this was a few years ago. Now he is at University and we seem to be doing fine again. In fact, he has become rather interesting. But then, I've gone back to University too. He says that it was him who drove me out of the house, and he says it was a good job he did, because look at me now. He might be right.

Audience: I had a similar experience with my son. And I have to say that although it is fine between us now, I am still sad about it. We lost the closeness we had, and I can't ever see it coming back. We were so close. I don't know if it was because I did something wrong, but there is a barrier between us now, and each time I see him it hurts me, to remember how close we were, and how guarded we seem to be now.

Audience: But perhaps that is necessary, if he is to find someone else to be close to. I had a rather mild version of that separation phase with my daughter. It was long ago now, but I can see that she was becoming a woman, and I was trying to keep her a child. She had to get away from me, to find her own self. Now that she has children of her own, we are close again, but I am careful, as I have been ever since that time, not to interfere too much in her life. That is very hard! But it works.

Darby: I think that what you say is true. The young person's need to break away is a natural response. It is nature demanding that we leave home and go out to find mates. It is the Soul of the World calling us to find someone who is somewhat familiar, but also foreign. Again, we look to tribal societies to see these calls of nature and soul. It seems that tribal societies are still close enough to nature to listen, but far enough away from nature to have to make rules and rituals to obey these natural laws. You cannot marry into your own family – too close, not enough diversity. But you cannot marry too far away from your tribe either, or you lose the protection of your people. To go too far is to create too much diversity.

Of course, these codes seem to break down in our multi-cultural cities. But they don't really, if you look close enough. If mother and son stay bonded through that period, the son is not freed from the past enough to go out and hunt a mate who is similar, yet different from his mother. Nature is not satisfied, and both mother and son pay a high price in the end. Saturn is demanding separation from the past and the progressed Moon is drawing one towards union with another who will be both familiar and unknown.

With mothers and daughters the story is somewhat different. Mothers giving birth to daughters give birth to themselves, or so it can seem. By the time of the Saturn and progressed lunar oppositions, the daughter is becoming a woman who herself will be able to give birth. She has to separate from her own source to become a source herself. Whether this is an easy or difficult separation depends on the two women involved. If she is lucky, the daughter will be able to move away from her mother in such a way that she can return again in a different way, at a later stage. In moving away she sees her mother very clearly – she sees the parts of her mother that she wants to disown in herself, and the parts of her mother she wants to have for herself.

Remember, each of these angles to the natal Moon returns you to your source and sends you away from your source. Mother and daughter reflect each other fully during this time, and what they each see in the mirror of each other is often somewhat disconcerting. "I don't want to be like her!" says the average daughter. "What is she becoming?" says the average mother. And more secretly, "How old I seem, next to her." This period demands a lot of wisdom, humour and patience from parents. If you haven't got it, you better get it. And it is different for every one of us.

Audience: I have a client who comes to me twice a year and he told me last month that he discovered that he was homosexual around the time of his Saturn opposition. He met a girl at his lunar opposition, and it was fine on the surface, but then he met her brother, and that was it! By his Saturn opposition he knew that he and the brother were attracted to each other in a way that really scared him. He said he had some bad years after that, until he was able to accept it. He's been in a relationship for twenty years now, and his lunar opposition is coming up again. He told me that he and his partner have a mutual woman friend and recently he noticed he was attracted to her! He has Moon in Sagittarius opposition Uranus in Gemini, from the 8th to the 2nd.

Darby: Is he frightened of this attraction?

Audience: He says not. He said he'll either do something about it or not. He was just interested in the timing when I told him about the cycle. You remember, we looked at it in my chart when I came to see you last year. My lover is a woman and we both discovered our same-sex sexuality around twenty-one, at the returning square. I've been following it with all my clients since then.

Darby: We'll go on to that one just now. The lunar opposition happens and then shortly after the Saturn opposition. Sometimes they are very close together, and sometimes three or more years apart. Between the one and the other each of us has undergone a change in relation to ourselves and to others around us. The lunar opposition opens us up to new possibilities in our relationship life. We are drawn to find reflection of our inner selves outside ourselves. The currents that are activated in our peer group affect us according to our own emotional natures. But one way or another we are pulled to find ourselves in others. By the Saturn opposition, the structure of our lives has changed because of the relationship we have made with others, and with those things outside ourselves which reflect the parts of ourselves that are emerging. The Saturn opposition shows us the restructuring that is taking place.

RETURNING SQUARE: MENDING WALLS

This phase comes around when you are around twenty-one years old. The Saturn square comes sometime after it, depending on how fast your progressed Moon is moving.

Audience: And this period coincides with the first square of transiting Uranus to natal Uranus.

Darby: Yes, this is the first hard angle of Uranus. The other two phases are awakenings too, but this is an Awakening.

Audience: Like the film, *Awakenings*.

Darby: And how many of us go to sleep again, having awoken to the impact of what life might really be about? The possibility, but also the responsibility. You have reminded me of a man I once knew. He told me that he thought most people have a brief moment of awakening around twenty-one, and then they progressively go to sleep the rest of their lives. Whenever he met anyone who was still "awake" in their thirties, forties, fifties, he was amazed. He said it was like seeing someone walking around in colour, in a black and white movie. It was both disturbing and exciting.

Let's look at Saturn first, this time. In our early twenties we are generally awakened to our potential usefulness and value in our society. This is the Saturn side of the story. The Saturn return will be the next major stage. We are now, here at twenty-one or so, on the final part of our journey towards becoming that which we are called to be: fully fledged members of our particular society. Some of us will become part of its centre, with all the materials and responsibilities that it implies – home, family, work in the world, clearly defined social networks. Others of us will find our place outside the walls of our society in one way or another. But very few of us are truly outside. We may be outside the gates, but we are still attached to the walls. This is the beginning of the phase that will direct us to our place.

We are considered adults now, in our society. If you have gone on to higher education, you are making decisions about the role you will take in the world. If not, you are in apprenticeship to something that will give you a place in the world. You may even already be very successful in your chosen work, but you are still a beginner, and have a very long way to go in the world before you are through. The next seven years, to the Saturn return, will show your ability to learn to cope with the demands of the world. By this I mean the necessity of living in society where you are expected to participate in such a way that you add to or maintain the wealth of your society, and that you take care of yourself, and any family you have. These are the years where you are expected to learn these things. Many women, in our society, will start having children, if they are not deeply vocated to something else.

Here the future is calling. We are moving towards it, towards the achievement of independence and the achievements required by our ego selves somewhere in the world. We are called to something that will give us purpose and structure. There is a sense of responsibility around it. Or perhaps it would be more accurate to say there is a necessity calling to us, and the pressure is on to find what this means for us. Our society looks at us with questions in its eyes, and we cannot avoid addressing some of those questions, even if it is only to ourselves and in secret.

Audience: These are still mostly Saturn issues, aren't they?

Darby: Yes they are. In the light of the Moon, we are also at a turning point. This begins with the progressed Moon square to natal Moon, some time before the Saturn square. And, once again, it brings new forms of relationship into our lives. Having lost our souls and found them again, in the light of relationships or art, beauty, music, we have arrived at another turning point. We have formed habits which give us the moments of eternity that we require for spiritual sustenance, though we may not recognise them as such. We have experienced our capacity to lose ourselves, some more than others. Having gone through one or another kind of fire, our inner natures call us to return to the container, the inner dwelling, which gives form to our power of reflection. Something returns us to the inner home we began to build at the first outgoing square, during our sixth or seventh year. Now, we attract relationships whose purpose, we might imagine, is to draw us inward so that we may discover ways to guard our souls – or perhaps it is to guard the dwelling in which our souls reside. If we are to enter the world with all its complex demands, we need a way of returning inwards when we must.

In the last phase we were drawn or driven to find reflection of ourselves outside ourselves. The progressed Moon at the incoming square reflects our need to find ways to return to our inner selves, if we are to navigate the world and all its multiplicity. Plotinus, the second century Neoplatonist, tells us that Soul puts lures in things by which we will be drawn, so that we can experience the longing for God. We are being lured by the world, and though we must respond to that, we also need inner walls strong enough to keep our souls alive within, so that we can be nourished by the eternal in the temporal.

Audience: Lures?

Darby: I always get into trouble when I use that word. There is always someone who wants to know what word Plotinus used for "lure." I think Marsilio Ficino might have used it, in his commentary on Plotinus. I know it is not Greek, and Plotinus did not say it this way. It's just that I remember it this way. Ficino, and before him Plotinus, described the process in such a way that it caught my imagination. Can't you see the Soul of the World casting lures, from your own soul, into certain things, certain people, at different times of life?

Plotinus says that you cannot want anything (or let us say here, anyone) whose shape or form is not already in your soul. And so these lines, these whispers of current, are drawn between you and another (thing, person), and your longing is activated. Thus does the Eternal draw us through the Temporal. Material, emotional longing is the time-space-bound dimension of eternal longing. Without this touch of eternity in one's day-to-day life, things become terribly flat.

Audience: There's always drugs, alcohol and sex.

Darby: You jest, but you're right! Each and all of these are direct gateways to eternity, sometimes very direct! You can see why so many cultures have ritualised their use so heavily, and why, when they are not contained in sacred space, drugs, alcohol and sex can become so destructive. Sex is the most powerful gateway of all given to ordinary mortals. We are all transported to eternal realms when we fall in love. At the most basic level, sex between two people of the opposite sex results, often enough, in the birth of another human being, which keeps the chain of time stretching into eternity. But all sexual attraction has the power for creation or destruction, and therefore partakes of something that is eternal, whether you act it out literally or not.

Back to our theme: In the previous phase, from when the progressed Moon was opposing natal Moon, we were being lured, or called out of ourselves. At the beginning of this incoming square, we are called, from within, to return to ourselves and reconnect with our souls in such a way that we will not get lost on our way into the world. Some people develop such strong walls around the place where their soul dwells, they seem to lose touch with themselves completely. Others, in beginning to hear the call of the world, the call of necessity and responsibility, try to retreat into the inner world of the timeless. Neither extremes really work.

Whatever relationships we are having at this time, whatever crises or dilemmas we encounter which activate our natal emotional pattern, these also give us the experience that will call for a new relationship to ourselves. As this happens some months before the incoming Saturn square to itself, it is a preparation for the external challenge which sets your sails towards your relationship to the world and its demands. Because it is the Moon, it is often hidden, in that you cannot see what is happening at the time. Only as the cycle progresses can you begin to see what the emotional turning was about. Of course the more distant you get from it, the clearer you can see. That is why it is easier to get perspective and wisdom after the second or even third returns of these phases.

Audience: I remember this period very well, and what I have noticed, astrologically, is that my Saturn square happened a year after my lunar square but it went on for about six months. I mean Saturn sat right on the square – direct to it, retrograde on it and direct again, all within two degrees. Can you say anything about the Saturn angle when it stops at the degree of your Saturn and just sits there for months? Is there anything we should know about that?

Darby: There probably is, but I'm not sure I know it. The progressed Moon never pauses. It keeps moving, by the nature of what it is. But Saturn, as well as all the planets, does sometimes just "hang around" as you say, in the 1° area. Let's see what arises if we think about this.

The Saturn angles are always uncomfortable, to one degree or another, because they represent successive stages of our development within the limitations of our temporal reality. Since our egos are very much embedded in this life in time, most of us feel the pinch of Saturn when it's time to adjust our ego position to a new stage of life. The various time spans for the Saturn angles are embedded in your chart from birth. At birth you could chart all the Saturn angles for the extent of your ephemeris! So it seems that certain angles are "destined" to be more demanding.

When Saturn moves through the angle without pausing, you can assume that the adjustment demanded is a simple one. But when it hovers for months, then you must trust that the adjustment between your ego position and the world you are entering requires greater depth of thought and attention. When you look back at that period again, try to see why it might have required a deeper working of your sense of identity and the requirements of your later position. The experience you got during that time must have gone quite deep and led to a profound reorientation of your life.

Audience: Yes it did. It was an extraordinary time of experience, and led me to becoming a psychotherapist at my Saturn return.

Darby: I think that if any of you look back at those angles, the ones that are longest, hardest, deepest, you will find that what was developing under the scaffolding was fairly permanent.

LUNAR RETURN: BEARING YOURSELF

The lunar return happens a year or so before the Saturn return. Uranus has trined its own place at twenty-seven, easing us into the changes that are about to happen. The Saturn return is not just a moment in time. It is a process that takes about eighteen months to two years. The Saturn return is a time in your life, not a day in your life. It is not the day that Saturn returns to itself, but the time around which this happens. Since the lunar return always comes some months before it, you might take that as the entry to your Saturn return.

So much has been written about the Saturn return. Many of you will have gotten into the study of astrology through reading Liz Greene's *Saturn*, written nearly twenty years ago. I don't want to say much about the Saturn return here, except to say that it coincides with developments in our lives which demand a re-evaluation of everything that has happened up until then. It often coincides with major changes in our lives. Our ego position is challenged. Our direction is challenged, and we make decisions which will effect the rest of our lives.

The weight of the world, with its "shoulds" and its "oughts", presses heavily on us. The pressure shows itself in the decisions we make during this time. The compass by which we navigate our lives is slowly settling onto a particular course, and we will follow that course, one way or another, for the next nearly thirty years. Transits of the outer planets will reveal the pathways which will open out to us, during this time.

It often feels like a rebirth, once the direction becomes clear. This feeling of rebirth has more to do with the progressed Moon than with the actual Saturn return. Saturn shows us the scaffolding that is being built to define the limits, or shall we say the boundaries, of our ego development. It is points us to our responsibility, our Necessity, if we are to fully experience this world into which we incarnated. It shows us where the development of self-discipline will bring us the greatest satisfaction; where we will suffer most for our irresponsibility; and where we will pay the greatest price for repression.

Audience: You said that we might see the lunar return as the entry to the Saturn return. Is it a preparation in any sense?

Darby: The lunar return gives birth to the one who is inhabiting this space – the one whose ego is being pressed into its role and its necessity. It is a preparation for the Saturn return only in that someone has to be there for something to happen. The lunar return, reflected in the emotional circumstances at the time, opens the gates to our deepest selves. These circumstances and our response to them reveal something fundamental about the nature of our soul's journey as it expresses itself through the dark and light, virtues and faults of our personality. And it reveals what sort of nourishment we truly seek from this life in matter and time – and, perhaps, what sort of nourishment we are truly fit to give to this life, in matter and time.

The lunar return is a preparation for the Saturn return, but the Saturn return can be seen as materialising the container for what comes forth at the lunar return. Container and contained: each is the yin and the yang to the other. Once you have seen them together you can never see one without the other.

Audience: I have just looked up the year and the month of my lunar return. It was fifteen years ago, but I remember it. I don't want to say anything about my circumstances then, but it was a time in which I discovered that I was not as fine a person as I had always thought. It never occurred to me before that I might not be a rather nice person. I wanted something at that time, and I have never been able to forget that I went for it, hurting several people quite badly on the way. I justified it to myself, of course, but I never quite got away with the justification. I still think about it.

Darby: Thank you for that. You have told us something quite significant here. Giving birth, as most of you know, is often a painful process. Whether it be a child, or a painting, or a book, a business, a computer program, or a true relationship, giving birth is fraught with danger. There are techniques we can learn, rituals we can practice to mitigate some of the unnecessary pain and danger, but birth is creation, and acts of creation bring us close to the eternal. It is very rarely clean. The lunar return reflects the time during which we give birth to our souls – or perhaps it is truer to say, our souls give birth to us – into a new dimension and a new self-awareness.

This self-awareness has many facets. Time and eternity intersect sharply, between the lunar and the Saturn return. We stand on a mountain and can see as far into the past as into the future. The circumstances and relationships of that time demand that we see deeply into our mortal nature, against the background of our immortality. We dare not hide from our own corruption and weaknesses, nor from the beauty at the centre of our beings. These will be reflected in our current circumstances and relationships. There are very clear moments between the lunar and the Saturn return. Some of them feel great, and some feel pretty dreadful. Discovering that you are not who you thought you were is part of it.

The Saturn return is about taking responsibility for your life, or at least beginning to see the depth of what that means. The lunar return, through its attending circumstances, shows who it is that you have to take responsibility for. You can't take responsibility for an abstract idea. The lunar return reveals your inner self, with all of its longings and its capacity to grasp for life's treasures.

Remember, it is the natal Moon's sign, position and aspects, which are being constellated. Your response to the relationships and circumstances of the lunar return reveals your basic nature, inherited through your ancestry and shaped by your life so far. The circumstances will differ from your physical birth twenty-seven and a half years ago, but the way you go after nourishment will be characteristically yours. Here you begin life again, with an inherited nature which has been lived and worked by you into what you are now.

Audience: I wasn't aware of going after anything I needed, but I think I got what I needed. For years and years I had felt guilty for not loving my mother. During the month of my lunar return she came to stay for two weeks. I had two small children, and she was there, ostensibly, to help. When she left I felt more exhausted than I ever imagined possible, but I also felt free. My husband came home that evening and found me lying dead beat on the couch, but humming the melody to "Hark the Herald Angles Sing."

Darby: She'd come for Christmas?!

Audience: No! It was September. And I am not even religious.

Darby: What had happened that made you feel so free?

Audience: I don't really know. I have natal Moon in Sagittarius in the 4th, conjunct Saturn...

Audience: Is Saturn before or after the Moon?

Audience: That's interesting. It is before the Moon, so the progressed Moon had already passed it – probably when I found out she was coming to visit! I got so depressed at the thought, but you always think it will be different this time. There are 6° between Saturn and the Moon. She lives in Australia, and she was coming to visit all her children, spending two weeks with each of us. But the sense of freedom! It might have been that I suddenly saw how extraordinarily selfish she was. She had always accused me of selfishness, and I can't deny it. But it was amazing to watch her over those two weeks. When she left I felt as though I would never feel guilty again, about anything or anyone.

Darby: And?

Audience: Well, of course that was a pipe dream. But I discovered that you may have to honour your father and mother, but you don't have to like them, if they are not likable.

Darby: The lunar return gave birth to a sense of freedom in your case. That may be unusual. If your mother is alive at the time it often indicates a change in your relationship with her. It is really a change in the nature of your relationship to life. It is birth into a new awareness. I have known many people who are deeply self-aware before their lunar return. At the lunar return, however, your emotional life reflects your depths in such a way that after that time, self-delusion is more and more likely to become self-indulgence.

Audience: That's putting it harshly.

Darby: I know it is. However, the relationships you have at the lunar return reflect your emotional nature in such a way that you are born to yourself. Every aspect of your emotional nature has been released or realised by now. Your progressed Moon has gone around your whole inner sky, and in doing so it has reflected every feeling and reaction that you are capable of. Now it starts its journey again, but this time you have an internal, living mirror in which to reflect your feelings, and the actions taken as a result of those feelings.

Audience: It sounds as if you are saying that the first time round you are making a mirror that can reflect, through every degree of the zodiac. At the lunar return it is complete and can begin to reflect clearly.

Darby: That's near it. Perhaps the word "making" is too concrete. "Evoking" might be better. Those moments where time and eternity intersect, when the past rises up through the present, are the moments in which this other dimension is evoked. By the lunar return, this dimension, this place of soul, is realised in such a way that it does begin to reflect clearly, whether you attend to it or not. For most of us it will take some time before we can interpret what we are seeing in that mirror, in our relationships, which are an important part of the body of that mirror. But the truth of our souls, eternal and incarnated in time, is there to be seen in all its colours.

From a practical point of view, this is a most auspicious time to begin to develop internal and external rituals which keep the mirror polished – rituals in which we ask ourselves questions which lead us always closer to our common humanity. Of course, one can always refuse to accept what the mirror is showing. Most of us have a bit of Snow White's stepmother in us. But our modern version is more like, "The ugliness I am seeing in this mirror is not mine. It is yours, his, hers." Then there is the opposite version: "The ugliness I am seeing in this mirror is all mine." These distortions can be seen through eventually. If you are willing to be patient and attend deeply enough, your personal emotional experiences can begin to show you the reflections of your own depths, which lead you to your common humanity and through to Nature and to the nature of life itself.

Now, as the progressed Moon goes round again, each moment in the cycle can return you to a time, just under twenty-eight years ago. When you arrive at the angles, there is a moment when each of these way-stations constellate the past in such a way that you can move into the future with greater depth of emotional perception. Through reflection and attention, your perceptions can take you through yourself and beyond yourself.

Audience: And all this all happens at the point of your lunar return?

Darby: Each of the points in the cycle that we are discussing today opens up a new phase of your life. The actual conjunction, square, or opposition coincides with an emotional event which opens up the next phase, but that phase develops over the next six or seven years.

Transiting outer planets and progressions of other planets will shape the story as it unfolds.

Audience: I only understood the implications of my lunar return about three years after it, even after my Saturn return. I began a relationship at the lunar return which was about to change my life, but I didn't know it at the time. It took me a few years to realise that the woman I met at my lunar return was the woman I'd been looking for since I was thirteen. She was so real and so true that I couldn't recognise her. I was too used to my fantasies.

Darby: It is so often easier to see in hindsight, which is most frustrating for astrologers, isn't it? Let's look at the second outgoing square to natal Moon. We still have a lot to do today, and I want to go through the cycle once more. I also want to show you the chart of someone who gave me the story of her life, so far, through looking at this and Saturn's cycle together.

The second cycle of the progressed Moon has the added dimension of the memories you bring to it. Because of your ability to go back in memory to the previous stage of your present progressed Moon, you have a bit more navigational power. In the first one, life is doing you. Once the Saturn return comes along, you are doing it with life.

I am going to spend very little time on each phase this time. I simply want to give you a feeling for the space. Those of you who are past your Saturn return all have the depth of memory to return to the earlier phase, and so you have everything you need to attend to each successive stage. By returning in memory to the previous time, your soul finds its own way to catch up to itself and to reorient itself. Attend to your memories with respect, and wait for your soul to catch up to itself.

The Saturn angle that follows the lunar angle will adjust the structure of your life and your ego to accommodate your inner development. The growing distance between the lunar and Saturn angles has its own story, and I shall try to address it another time.

SECOND CYCLE, FIRST SQUARE: RELINING YOUR NEST

A few years before the second outgoing Saturn square, the progressed Moon reaches its outgoing square position. It happens between thirty-two and thirty-four. The outer planet activity is minimal during this angle. Uranus is quincunx its own place at some point, but the general disruption is less than at most angles. Having said this, I haven't noticed that this period is less significant than any of the others.

At the lunar return there was a rebirth in terms of our relationship to others, to life and to ourselves. The Saturn return seemed to fix our position, and whether we like it or not, give us a status in our community. Now this position is challenged. Once again, as at the first outgoing square, around six or seven, there is an inner reorientation. Your sense of belonging and your sense of isolation are brought out by the emotional events of the time. The relationships that are central to you during this time reflect where you have been, and where you are headed in a particularly potent way.

You may feel cut off from eternity, or, if you are more practical, you feel something lacking. During this time you are drawn to people who point you to the place where the next stage of your emotional development lies. Through these people your inner dwelling place is revisited. One way or another you are brought back to the place which you first claimed in your sixth or seventh year under the first square. Whatever inner or outer conflict is constellated during this time, it pulls you inward – to reline the nest, you might say. There is a new dimension emerging, and it calls for a new relationship to life.

In the first seven years of your life you were drawn away from eternity into time. During the lunar return, at twenty-seven, time and responsibility deepened through experience, and you were born again. Now, at this outgoing square, deeper nourishment is needed, and it is your current emotional relationships which show you both the lack of such nourishment and the possibility of finding it.

At this point you are drawn back to your roots, to where you have come from. The past returns and demands a review. Whoever is currently central to your emotional landscape brings you experiences which set off your natal relating pattern, but also open up new inner chambers which need to be inhabited. The past and the future pull you, each in their own way.

Audience: This reminds me that Jupiter is exalted in Cancer. Whatever visions you have of the future, whatever potential, if it is to be real, must come out of your history, your past. Nothing that you create or become can really satisfy you if it is not from your deepest self. Everything else is someone else's dream.

Darby: Yes, that's a lovely way of expressing it. Exaltation positions of the planets hint at so much, don't they? All of this work we are doing today with the progressed Moon is contained in that one astrological fact: Jupiter is exalted in Cancer. And all of Nature hides in those words.

The emotional circumstances of your present situation bring up the ghosts of your ancestors. You go down as far as the cord will take you. At the lunar return you connected with your roots and were sent on your way again. Now, at this point these roots release their ghosts to meet the incoming promise of the future. Your soul reorients itself, and to do that it must feel the past and the future at once. It often coincides with a time during which you seek a new tribe who will better reflect your inner world. You are looking for a place to belong. When the Saturn incoming square happens a few years later, your emotional base has been established, and structural work goes on in your life which will reflect the inner development of the lunar square.

Audience: Why are transiting Saturn angles to its natal position so uncomfortable, and sometimes even more than when it contacts personal planets?

Darby: I don't know. But I agree with you. It can feel as though someone is scraping off years of calcification from the drainpipes in your psychic body.

Audience: Maybe that's because that's what is happening.

Darby: Maybe. And once the calcification has been scraped off, the next stage of life can begin.

SECOND CYCLE OPPOSITION: FALLING IN LOVE AGAIN

Darby: From an astrological point of view, the early forties are pretty loaded, aren't they?

Audience: The Neptune square.

Audience: And isn't the Pluto square somewhere in there?

Darby: It is for people born around 1950. Earlier for those born after, and later for those born earlier.

Audience: The Uranus opposition and the Saturn opposition.

Darby: And somewhere in all of this, between forty and forty-two, the lunar opposition. So many cycles are at points of intersection around the time we turn forty. And it isn't surprising that we find this birthday somewhat daunting. It is more surprising to find people who don't seem to be stirred up by it. Once again, we are in a period which can look like rebellion. This time, the challenge is not so much to the parents, or the mother, but is to those we are closest to at the time.

It is particularly interesting when it coincides with having teenage children at the same point in their cycles. They are at their first opposition and seeking their emotional nourishment from a world unknown to their parents, at the same time the parent is seeking nourishment from a life which is in opposition to that which was happening at the child's birth. So both parent and child are new to each other. For those who are secure, this can be a delightful rediscovery and a mutual opening out to life. To those who are insecure, either at the time, or in general, it can be disturbing or frightening. And for men and women who haven't had children, it usually demands an inner confrontation, where the past and its longings are released and the unknown and unpredictable future is opened.

Once again it can seem as though one's soul is flung outside oneself, and you have to go and find it. It won't be found in the familiar territory that you have established inside yourself. Returning, in memory, to the time of the first opposition will help you catch up to yourself by helping you identify the feelings that might be underneath your actions at the time. The things that were happening at the time will have been circumscribed by the transiting outer planets to your personal planets, as well as progressions of other planets. The circumstances of this progression will be circumscribed by very different transits and progressions.

At the first opposition, the relationship between you and your mother was challenged. This time there may be a bit of that, but at this age, one's closest relationship is not usually one's mother. If it is, then there will be a challenge to it again – a need to get free, from the depths of one's self. There will be a need to reach out into the unknown. And for the rest of us, the need to reach out into the unknown is there, too.

Relationships formed during this time call out parts of yourself that have been dormant for a long time. The necessities of life, the responsibilities and demands that are attached to the choices you made during or just after your Saturn return, have channelled your emotional nature in a particular way. During the lunar opposition your emotional nourishment may seem to drain away from your normal day-to-day activity. People encountered at this time set off a longing for a new experience. What you do about that will be decided between the lunar opposition and the coming Saturn opposition.

Audience: After I phoned you last week, and you told me what you would be covering in this seminar, I made a list of all the dates of the lunar and Saturn angles up to now. I have noticed, as you've been going along here, that I seem to be always a bit slow. I can connect what you are saying with each transition, but not exactly on time. The people I meet who set off the new phase come into my life later, sometimes a year or two after the actual aspect.

Darby: I know it seems that way. I have looked very carefully at that too. Like you, I can see the significant relationships or circumstances sometimes a year, or even two, after the actual month of the angle. We are dealing with the Moon here, and so much of the time we are in half-light or less. But if you keep a record of the events and the people encountered during the actual month of the angle, when you look back you may see the traces of the emotional development that shows its brighter colours later. There will be a moment when past and present meet in a particularly significant way. That turning will open you to a new phase of your inner development, a new phase of your relationship to life on earth. The Moon's realm is a secret hidden thing much of the time. Sometimes things are lit up gloriously by its light, but rarely. Most times we only get glimpses.

INCOMING SQUARE:
MENDING WALLS AND WINDOWS

This angle occurs around forty-eight or forty-nine, around the time of Uranus quincunx to itself. The Saturn square will not happen until fifty-one or so, but there is something that happens between them that may give us a clue to this part of our journey through life.

Audience: Maybe the lunar square prepares you for becoming fifty and the Saturn square confirms it by certain harsh realities that become obvious. Like, some kid stands up for you on the bus at the lunar square, but it's not until the Saturn square that you notice that they start helping you across the street!

Audience: Where do you live where kids are so chivalrous?

Audience: I was speaking metaphorically.

Darby: But I think you've got something there. What astrological event happens at fifty?

Audience: The Chiron return.

Darby: Yes. At fifty we have our Chiron return. It is contained within the lunar and Saturn incoming square. What happens at the lunar level is often unrecognised by one's day-self. What happens at the Saturn square is more easily recognised, if only because it is clearly uncomfortable! The Chiron return is a great turning point in one's life, which seems to reveal one's mortality and one's immortality, both at the same time, in such a way that one is caught between feeling very old and very young again.

Audience: It shows you how frail you are and boosts your engines at the same time. At least it did that for me, but nothing else astrological was happening, and I could really experience it. I remember thinking that the wound of Chiron was simply that we are mortal, or something like that. It hit me in such a way that I suddenly felt immortal at the moment I really knew I was mortal. It was exhilarating.

Darby: Do you remember the lunar angle before it?

Audience: Yes. I checked it before coming here today. The month of the previous lunar square – about a year before my fiftieth birthday – my daughter had her first child. I became a grandmother.

Darby: And past and present came together in a way that opened up a new phase of your life. This stage returns us to the previous one at around twenty-one. At that time one is entering the field called "the world," and so there is a natural move to guard one's soul, even if this happened deep beneath the surface of one's awareness. There is a similar move here, but perhaps we can say it is a return to one's inner dwelling place to renovate or renew one's relationship with one's soul – that part of oneself which lives in eternity and lives in time. Can you tell me how that might have constellated the need to guard this inner self?

Audience: I wonder if this is connected to it? I remember being very, very aware that I must be careful to establish the right relationship with my daughter, her husband and their baby. I had seen too many women mess it up right from the beginning, pretending to help but getting in the way, offering advice that was not wanted, interfering in all sorts of ways. I thought to myself, "Be cool now, go slow." Perhaps that was the way this phase manifested in me. I have natal Moon in the 8th and my progressed Moon was in the 5th at the time. I know that I can be so aware of the deeper feelings in other people that I become completely insensitive to what they want or need from me.

Darby: These angles always coincide with relationship events. They aren't always as powerful as the birth of a grandchild, and they are usually better seen in hindsight. This turning time expresses itself in some relationship move that lets one's inner self know that a reorientation is happening. The natural inclination is to go inward and check the walls of one's container so that self-containment becomes comfortable. But the windows of this inner dwelling place are important too, and they must be still be able to open to life's unpredictability. In about seven years the second lunar return will occur.

SECOND LUNAR RETURN

The progressed Moon returns to its natal position around the age of fifty-four. The second Saturn return will not happen for another four or even five years. We know that the second Saturn return demands that we look very carefully at the structure of our lives, and prepare in some way for old age. This need arises out of our inner or outer lives, depending on our natures.

Some people require events to occur that show them the necessity of preparing for their old age in some way. It is the ways in which this happen that are characteristic to each of us. And each person has a different way of facing this confrontation. Some people do not need outer events to direct them to their own mortality. They are sensitive to the inner changes that are pointing to the place where attention must be brought.

The lunar return, which happens usually four or even five years before, brings you into a new emotional relationship with those around you. Again, this can coincide with the birth of grandchildren. Whatever emotional experience you are having during this time prepares you for the rest of your life. You have time to get used to it here, because the Saturn square is a way off. You are allowed, it seems, to grow into your new relationship with life.

I have a friend whose mother died recently at her third lunar return. She was irritated by her mother a lot of her life, but she told me that it was a shattering experience. I can imagine it was, if your mother has been alive all your adult life and even into the early years of your old age.

I can't say much about this period. Of course I have had clients going through their second lunar and Saturn return since I began my practice so many years ago. But I have not attended the lunar side of it in the same way as I have the Saturn side. Because the Moon is about feelings, I have not felt as though I could reach into it until I have gone through it myself. And I have not reached this stage yet.

I only know that it is a rebirth, at the emotional level. You have completed an entire cycle of your emotional life and your soul is ready to engage with its relationship to time and eternity in a new way. Returning to your previous lunar return and to your birth in your imagination, remembering these moments, allows you to catch up to yourself and to be open to the next stage of your soul's life in time. Attending it with care and respect gives you the chance to be open to the emotional relationships that will take you into old age, which is your gateway back to eternity. Going back in time can return you to your source, which opens the door to your deeper source.

I'm not going to talk about the third round of this cycle this time. But I will tell you about a dear friend who died recently at the age of eighty-four. Her third return, in Libra, had been a few years before her death. She was a Sagittarian and a great traveller, with both her body and her mind. We looked at the overall aspects for the year of her lunar return and they were pretty good, so she decided to go to China for a visit. She was a painter, and she had always been fascinated with China, and she said it might be the last chance she'd ever get to go so far on her own.

So she did, and when she returned we talked about how such a long trip felt, to her, like a preparation for death, which was an even longer trip. So many things she did after that seemed like a last time. She even did a stunning collage of a sunset, which she said might be her last one. When death finally came for her, she fought it, even though she had been preparing for it. At the time I was sad about that, because she suffered in her battle, but now I have learned that we each have our own relationship with death, as we do with life, and to decide whether another person's relationship is good or bad can be trying to play God.

Each lunar return is a birth. In the case of my friend, the first lunar return coincided with the birth of her first child. I am not sure about the second one – can't remember the details at this moment – but the third took her to the farthest place she could imagine, and gave birth to the idea of the longest journey she could imagine, her own death.

She began to emotionally prepare herself at the lunar return. While it progressed through Scorpio, she went through a great deal of loss and fear. During that time she said to me, "I am in hell." I hated seeing her suffer so. I said, "Your progressed Moon is in Scorpio so perhaps it is purgatory." She thought for a bit and said, "Perhaps it is." She died just as her progressed Moon went into Sagittarius, and her death was peaceful. She flew out of her body, and returned to her source, which, for us, is the realm of the eternal.

CHAPTER 9

An Individual Chart

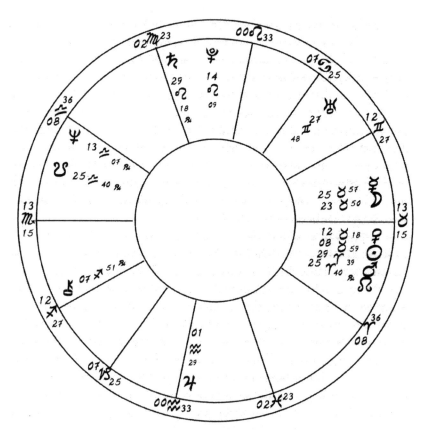

"Helen"
29 April 1949, 5:50pm (15:50GMT), Johannesburg, SA (26S15, 28E00)
Koch cusps

Now we shall look at the chart of a woman and follow the lunar cycle through her life, up to now. She is forty-five years old. I shall call her Helen.

We met in 1976 in South Africa, and she visited me recently in London. During her stay we discovered that we had met during the month of her lunar return. That led us to go back and trace the progressed Moon as it formed its angles to the natal position. This brought in the Saturn cycle quite naturally, as she has a natal square between them. She has a good memory and could remember the dates of events in her life. In many cases she could remember the actual months, or near enough, of either the lunar angle or the Saturn angles, and when I asked her if I could use her chart in this seminar she agreed.

The Moon-Saturn square in her chart will, on the one hand, make it easier to see the connection between the lunar and Saturn cycle. On the other hand, you won't see how linked the two cycles are, even when they aren't by natal aspect. But I hope this will encourage you to track the two cycles in your own chart so that the connection between the two becomes a fundamental part of your own observation of charts.

Let's look at the chart itself for a moment. Helen has Sun, Moon, Venus, and Mercury all in Taurus. Her Sun is conjunct Venus in Taurus on the cusp of the 7th house. The Sun is in the 6th house, square Jupiter in Aquarius at the roots there, and it is close to Venus just on the cusp of the 7th house.

The Sun-Venus conjunction is square to Pluto in the 10th house. Venus, in Taurus and ruler of the Taurus Sun, is quincunx Neptune in the 12th. Scorpio is rising, and Pluto, the transpersonal ruler of the chart, is the most elevated planet. The Moon is conjunct Mercury in the 7th and both are square to Saturn in the 10th house. Mars, the personal ruler of the chart, is in Aries in 6th house, trine to Saturn and square to Jupiter.

Audience: Her Mars and her Venus are both in their own signs, and Venus is on the cusp of one of its own houses. They must tell a powerful story.

Darby: Yes, they do. Mars is in quite good condition, being trine to Saturn and sextile to Uranus. It is square to Jupiter. All the members of her family have Mars-Jupiter contacts. It seems to represent the unsettled nature of the family background. Her parents were German Jews who fled Nazi Germany. They were new to South Africa when she and her brother were born. Her Venus in Taurus on the 7th cusp is square to Pluto. Her parents were in personal crisis during her infancy. In her adult life these planets have expressed themselves clearly. She is extremely adventurous and daring, at times reckless, and spends a lot of time in the African bush, exploring various internal and external territories, and this is a very happy side of her life. She really has fun adventuring, and is not afraid of hard trekking – by this I mean she does not shy away from trips that involve hard work. Her relationship life has been difficult. She has had very intense relationships which seem to have sharply defined lifespans, and there have been long gaps between significant relationships. As she would say, "Difficult lessons to learn."

She had an older brother who was born in 1947. She was born in 1949, and eighteen months later her father fell in love with someone else and left home. With her Moon, Mercury and Venus all in the 7th house, whatever happened to her mother and her brother and, of course, her father – the Sun is conjunct Venus there – registered very strongly in her infant body and psyche.

The 7th house Moon tells us that her mother's ability to attend to her at the time depended a lot on what was happening with her husband. For better or worse, this child was entangled with her parental relationship. And she was a factor in their relationship. Her father was only gone for a few months, but I think her mother's feelings during that time must have impressed her very deeply. Her Moon-Mercury square Saturn tells us that her mother may have been suppressing the expression of her feelings for social reasons, but this child not only felt them but was deeply affected by them.

In any case, he came back, and they went on and in the end seemed to have quite a good marriage, all things considered. But at the time Helen was born he felt very lost. She has Sun and Venus square Pluto, and she was born to a father who was in a period of darkness. He had terrible loss behind him – all of his family in the holocaust and recent, personal confusion and loss. He did not know where he stood in terms of his life, his work, his family, his marriage. He was a Cancerian with Moon in Pisces conjunct Uranus in the 4th. He had six planets in water and Scorpio rising. Can you imagine how lost he must have felt?

Her mother was unhappy in her new country, lonely and feeling very much unconnected to her environment. She had lots of planets in the 11th house and Mercury in Capricorn in the 10th house. She had a very strong awareness of what other people think, and she was new to that country and had two small children, and her husband left her. Helen's planets in the 7th house with their aspects tell us that she absorbed a large amount of their trauma.

She told me that at 18 months old she got hold of a bottle of sleeping pills and ate a lot of them. When she told me this, she laughed and said, "I tried to kill myself at 18 months old." She doesn't remember the incident, but her mother certainly did. Apparently she was unconscious for three days. Can you imagine how terrifying it must have been for her mother? This child had natal Moon in the 7th house, so you can see clearly here how deeply she must have been connected with her mother's relationship to her father. At this time, Helen's progressed Moon was in the 8th house. Her mother was in a deep marital crisis. There were also financial problems, and her eighteen-month-old daughter nearly kills herself. This child was reflecting her mother's fear and distress in an extreme manner.

Audience: Do you know where her mother's progressed Moon was?

Darby: I don't remember the exact degree, but I do know it was in the 12th house. Her mother had natal Moon opposite Saturn, and her child had natal Moon square Saturn. Both of them have Saturn in Leo – mother's in the 5th house and daughter's in the 10th house. The feelings around at that time were not being expressed directly. They came out in this rather darkly dramatic way.

Audience: I want to ask another question about that Sun-Venus square Pluto…

Darby: I'm sure you do, but at this point I'd rather unfold her story without diversions. I will try to answer your questions as I go along, indirectly, rather than directly. I am not showing you this chart to penetrate its secrets – I am showing it to you so that you can see how one person has developed through her lunar and Saturn cycles.

After a few months, her parents were reunited. They stayed together the rest of their lives and their marriage grew into one where affection and consideration were expressed. The dark dimensions between them rarely opened up again in such a way as to affect her directly.

When she was six years old, her **progressed Moon** was in Leo in the 10th house, and it was at its first angle, **squaring its own place** in the 7th. I asked her what happened and she told me that she started school, about a month before the exact angle. I asked her how she liked it. She said, "I absolutely loved it." A few months after the angle, her progressed Moon conjoined Saturn. I asked her if she could remember anything with her mother during that period. She said, "Nothing I can remember." I waited for a bit, wondering how to find a reflection of the progressed angle, which, in her case involved Saturn, and then she said, "The only thing I remember that wasn't so nice was that I had two best friends, and we used to gang up on each other, and two would pick on one. I was always with the two, until one time I was the one, and the other two ganged up on me. They threatened to torture me." She described to me what they threatened to do, which I will not charm you with at this point. She remembers being absolutely terrified.

As I have told you, both her parents were Jewish refugees. As teenagers each of them had fled Nazi Germany, sent away by their parents, and most of the rest of the family had been killed in the Holocaust. When she told me about the torture threat, it reminded her of something else. She remembered that her first years at school were tainted by a secret fear. Her parents were obviously German, but none of the family looked Jewish, and she was afraid that if people thought she was not Jewish, they would think her parents were Nazis – that she was a Nazi. We forget how deeply children think and feel at times, we forget what they pick up from adult conversations, don't we? Each of us forms ourselves by how we take things that circulate around us into our psyches. She did not speak about this to anyone at the time. We see the Sun-Venus square to Pluto resonating here.

She said the threat of torture "made a big impression" on her, but the rest of the time she was having a pretty good time. Her Moon is square to Saturn, and people with this aspect are not generally given to expressing or even knowing their own emotional waves. They are brought up to suppress the natural flow of emotions, and so painful things have to be dug out for them to remember. She said that, in spite of these darker memories, she felt as though she came into her own when she went to school. She said, "Getting away from home, I got a life of my own." Getting away from home, and away from her mother's constant presence, she began to build a life for herself, which involved relationships with others. You can see the Jupiter in Aquarius at the roots of the chart. She apparently started bringing friends home very early. She filled the house with their liveliness. She belonged to different gangs of kids at different times. She was finding her own tribe and digging out a container for her own soul.

A year after the lunar square, **Saturn squared its own place**. We are looking at Saturn here as describing ego development in the world. It is the urge towards mastery that develops self-respect and earns the respect of others. She said that she remembers this Saturn square clearly. She had written an essay and she was really excited about it. She was sure it would get accepted by the school paper and be published. However, to her shock, her best friend's essay was picked out for publication and hers was not. I asked her what her essay had been about. She told me that she couldn't remember, but she remembered the essay her friend had written. It was called "Mrs. Mouse."

Audience: The shock must have occurred when Uranus was semi-sextile its own place, in the 9th house of publication.

Darby: Nearly. That semi-sextile had happened a few months before, and now Uranus had gone into Leo and was opposing her Jupiter in the 4th house. Same theme there. In any case, she made a major decision at that time, at the age of seven. She said, "I decided, 'I will never be noticed. I will never let this happen again.'" Have you noticed how powerful these decisions of Scorpio rising people are? When they make emotional decisions there is such a force behind them.

She told me it was not until Saturn was in Scorpio again, twenty-nine years later, that she felt she had really managed to undo that decision. She said that she had, of course, always wanted to be noticed, but she went underground for a very long time before she began to realise this. We'll see that later. I think the power of that time and that decision must have been so great because transiting Pluto was also conjunct her Saturn! You see how things fill out when we look at the other astrological events.

The next phase began for her at twelve and a half. Her **progressed Moon**, in Scorpio, **opposed its own place**, in Taurus. It was moving fast through her chart in her early years. She told me that she experienced an intense rebellion against her mother. She said, "I looked at her one day and hated her."

She told me it happened in an instant. She was in the garden, and one of the garden tools had got lost. Her mother blamed her.

She knew she had not touched it, and asked the gardener to confirm this. He, fearing blame himself, denied her his support. Her mother believed the gardener. And she went on to criticize her for other things, her hair and her manner of dressing. Her mother said she looked bad to the neighbours; she'd dyed it orange or green or some such colour. It was 1961, after all! Helen looked at her mother and thought, "You'll never have power over me again." She turned against her mother. Then at fourteen, **Saturn opposed its own place;** from Aquarius in the 4th house to natal Saturn in Leo in the 10th house. She said, "I became really obnoxious." At school a teacher shouted at her. She felt attacked. She looked at him and she thought "You are just a person, you're not anything special. And I'm a person too. I don't have to listen to you at all." Any conscious respect she had for authority was finished. She only looked to her friends now for recognition and respect.

Now this person is extremely charming and graceful. This was not her most charming and graceful moment. Just after that she changed schools, and she felt as though she had been set free. Uranus was trine her Sun during that period. Also, her progressed Sun came to conjoin her natal Moon. She said she felt wonderful.

At the end of 1968, her **progressed Moon**, in Aquarius, came into the **incoming square**, to her natal Moon. It was on its way to the opposition of Saturn in Leo in the 10th. She wrote her matriculation and entered university. She took drama. I was surprised at this. With Saturn in Leo in the 10th house, square the Moon and also square to Mercury, and with Scorpio rising, she became a drama student. I said, "What?" She said, "I know, weird."

Audience: She was going for the recognition that she had denied herself. Somewhere it had to surface again.

Darby: Yes it did. But again, it did not have a happy conclusion. She said it was the loneliest time of her life. I looked at the major transits. She had transiting Neptune at 24° of Scorpio. It was in opposition to her natal Moon-Mercury conjunction, and also setting off the natal square to Saturn in the 10th. Her earlier resolve to never be noticed was working against her desire to be noticed. She said that she felt as though she was drowning. She said, "I would have killed myself, but I didn't have the energy." Lucky for the rest of us, because she would have been a loss to a lot of people, although she didn't know it at the time. She was at that stage when the progressed Moon squares its own place, on its way back to natal Moon. If you remember, this is the time when your soul finds ways to protect itself as the demands of the world begin to call. Her experiences at drama school drew her inwards, to find a place of relative safety. Her early conditioning was harsh, and so the search for that place was difficult, as her inner home territory, in terms of this life, was not comfortable.

Soon after, **Saturn had its third square**, the incoming square. In her chart, this means that Saturn was on her Moon-Mercury and squaring its own place in Leo. She quit drama school, and in November 1971, six months after the exact square, she began training to be a nurse. The Sun in the 6th was beginning to show its light. A few months later, she met a man, fell in love, and they began living together. Her progressed Moon moved into her 5th house, on its way towards the lunar return. Saturn was now in the 8th house. The relationship lasted three and a half years, ending mid-1975. The last year of it was very painful. When she completed her training she went off to Australia, with Saturn transiting the 9th house, and she got a nursing job there. Her progressed Moon was conjunct the Sun, then Venus and then square Pluto. She had a terrible and lonely time in Australia and started developing a serious eating disorder. She returned around her twenty-seventh birthday, in May of 1976.

In June of that year she had her **lunar return**. That was the month we met, for the first time. It was a significant meeting for both of us, for various reasons. Because it was her lunar return, it was the time of an emotional rebirth. She had completed a whole cycle of emotional experiences that arose out of her conditioning, but deeper than that too. We are not only products of our conditioning. We go back too far in time for that to be true. She had completed a cycle of emotional experience that gave shape to her life, gave her a story. Now she was to begin again, this time taking part in the writing of the story, as it unfolded through her.

This person she met that month happened to be me, an astrologer, and that was rare enough in South Africa at the time. She was fascinated by the world she encountered through meeting astrology. She remembered the date of our meeting. It was the 8th of June 1976. It was the day of her Mercury return. The nodes were on her Ascendant-Descendant axis; South node on her Descendant-Venus. Jupiter was in Taurus and would be conjoining her Moon-Mercury within a month. We met in a restaurant.

Audience: Of course it was a restaurant.

Darby: Why?

Audience: All that Taurus.

Audience: It could have been a paddock.

Audience: Or a garden.

Audience: With the Moon conjunct Mercury it could have been a really nice train.

Audience: The restaurant car of a very nice train, stopped in a field.

Darby: Does anyone know the degree on the Ascendant at the moment? Lunacy rising here. It would have been splendid if it had been the restaurant car of a very nice train. We had some incredibly nice trains in South Africa. But it was a very good Greek restaurant in Johannesburg and, Mercury honoured, she was introduced to me by her brother. Does that satisfy you? Her brother was a friend of mine, and she had just come back from Australia, and he wanted us to meet. He thought we would like each other. And we did. We had a fine time and began a friendship over a Greek meal.

Audience: What did you eat?

Darby: I don't have Moon in Taurus. I could ask her. She might actually remember. She did remember something about the food, because when we were going back over this meeting she said to me, "You didn't notice that I didn't eat, did you?" I hadn't noticed. I had been interested in her impressions of Australia, and enjoyed the way she expressed herself. She told me later that she had a big food problem at that time. It had started in Australia and continued to plague her for many years, all during the early years of our relationship. She kept it very secret, as people did in the 1970s. Anorexia and bulimia were not recognised as such in the 1970s, not in South Africa, anyway. Also, with her Scorpio rising and Saturn square Moon, she was naturally secretive.

During this time she became a midwife, and she began hanging around with someone who talked astrology all the time, and she began to pick it up, in a Moon-in-the-7th kind of way. Two years later she had her **Saturn return**. But in the two years between, her progressed Sun and Moon came together.

It was in August of 1977, and they conjoined at 6° Gemini. When that happened she began to work with something called Lifeline. Do you have Lifeline? It is an organisation where people phone up in distress, and you are a responsive and sympathetic voice on the end of the line.

Audience: We have the Samaritans.

Darby: Of course. Within a few months of joining, her progressed Moon went into the 8th house. When it was there the first time she nearly killed herself. The second time it went in she joined a group of people working to help people who felt like killing themselves. In August of 1978, just a month after her Saturn return, she had an accident. The car went across the highway, turned around six times and landed in a tree upside down. It was very traumatic for everyone in the car, but no one died. She broke her leg and had various other injuries, and she had to go to bed for three months. With her Mars in Aries square to Jupiter, she was restless and bored, so I bought her some astrology books, as she said she'd like to use the time to really come to grips with the language.

That was when astrology really happened for her. Most of you know that moment. You read a certain book on astrology, and thud! You're hooked. Did I mention that Uranus was on her Ascendant in Scorpio at the time? No? I think it should be mentioned, don't you? Isn't it perfect sometimes?

She had enjoyed our conversations up to then, but this was different. I wasn't around all the time during those three months and so I didn't really know that was happening. But by the beginning of 1979, I noticed. Before that time I would say something astrological and she would say, "What does that mean?" After that she was saying things like, "Isn't it interesting that he has the Sun square his Moon opposite his Jupiter, and he is moving countries again." From then on she was talking the language and using it, to understand other people and herself, and to seek understanding about her relationship life.

Within a year after her Saturn return, she joined an organisation which was dedicated to personal growth. This sort of trend was growing in South Africa, and she got involved. She'd had no significant relationships with men since the one that ended in 1975. We had become close friends, and through our friendship she opened up her astrological mind. By the end of 1979 my life had taken me somewhere else. She experienced this as loss, and felt betrayed for a time. However, by now, she had begun to look at herself objectively, and to see a pattern in her life around close relationships. She set off on a journey that brought her a new vocation and a new world of people. She met someone who would become, over time, a very close friend and with whom she would share an extraordinary range of experiences.

Audience: I have Moon in the 7th house in Gemini, and my whole life seems to be lived in terms of my closest relationship. It doesn't seem to matter whether I am happy or sad in a relationship, but when I don't have one, I am desolate. I thought that was because it was in Gemini. But I wonder, is this the same for her?

Audience: She does have the Moon conjunct Mercury.

Darby: I do think it is simply the Moon in the 7th. One's soul life is brought alive by relationship. One incarnates into this material realm attuned to the waves that flow between oneself and another. When the Moon is aspected by Saturn or Pluto, then there are naturally times when one's emotional life seems to dry up. And then one either has to work or to wait until new levels of relationship open up. As she developed her astrological awareness, I learned this through her understanding of her own experience. She was able to articulate her feelings – Moon conjunct Mercury in trine to Jupiter in Aquarius – as she began to understand it. Recently she said to me, "Relationship is stony ground for me, but I am discovering I can move on stony ground in a way that is natural for me." Isn't that a rich image for the Moon in Taurus square to Saturn?

In June of 1983, her **progressed Moon** was in Leo, at the **outgoing square** to its own natal position in Taurus. By now she had become so involved in the organisation that she was virtually running it. She was involved with training, although she was not a trainer, and she had a whole new world of people through her friendship. The particular friend she had made in 1980 had become a strong relationship.

If we look back at the first time her progressed Moon was in this position, when she was six, we see that this was a time where she made lots of friend but got scapegoated. She wrote that essay and got hurt by Saturn's realm, and made the decision to not go for visibility. This was a way to contain her soul and keep herself protected.

During this present phase, she was running the office of her organisation – good Sun in the 6th stuff, and Mars there too – and now she wanted to become a trainer, which would mean high visibility. She remembered the decision she had made as a child, when she was at this same lunar angle. Now she wanted to become visible. She decided that she had to overcome her childhood decision and she'd have to work at it: Moon square Saturn setting to work on its emotional responses. So, as she put it to me, she did everything in her power to undo the spell which she had put on herself. She was absolutely passionate to achieve visibility. It seemed to her that this was important work on herself, and since she was in an organisation whose aim was self-development and self-awareness, this was the time and the place to do it.

Her progressed Moon was in Leo, moving between its natal square and the conjunction with Saturn. Transiting Saturn was sextiling her natal Saturn from Libra to Leo. Neptune was in Sagittarius, trining natal Saturn. She was working very hard to rework her habitual responses to people in authority, and to give herself the chance to express her own temporal (Saturn) and spiritual (Neptune) authority. Her relationship with her mother was still fraught with difficulties and resentments, but suddenly her mother became ill, and Helen felt deeply that she had to take care of her. She looked at her own Moon square Saturn and wrote to me saying, "Wouldn't this happen? That Moon square Saturn! I spend my whole life getting away from my mother, and now it looks like I am going to have to take care of her the rest of her life." This turned out to be true. But she took on the responsibility with all the strength of her willing heart. It was a very rocky road at the beginning. And, before this period ended, she discovered that her close friend was beginning to sabotage her efforts to become a trainer.

She fought to get into the position in the organisation that she wanted, and she did not exclude any of the emotional events around her from her inner work.

Audience: What do you mean?

Darby: I mean she didn't say, "Here I am trying to overcome my early struggles, and my mother has to get ill and distract me. And now my friend is betraying me, so how can I possibly achieve my goal?" She included these events as part of the process. Everything that happened she saw as part of the emotional equation and worked to get clear with herself and others. Most admirable.

By the time **Saturn** was in Scorpio, **squaring its natal position** in Leo she had achieved it. This was 1985. She was running courses. She was visible and she felt she had overcome her childhood decision. She had confronted her friend again and again, and they had worked through it and were closer than ever. She was faithfully attending her mother, who was an invalid now, and clearing every difficulty between them as they arose. She was being this Saturn square Moon-Mercury, not simply being an effect of the feelings that arose out of its meaning.

Audience: What about her relationship with men? You keep mentioning her friendships with women, but you haven't said if these were sexual relationships.

Darby: Her friendships with women weren't sexual, and she had not had a sexual relationship with a man since 1975. She had become very practical about this, with all those Taurus planets, and she had decided that since it wasn't happening, she would enjoy the relationship possibilities that life offered her. Her friendship life was a rich source of nourishment for her, and for those with whom she shared this gift of friendship. I don't think I have ever known anyone so practical in this way, certainly not in my Neptune in Libra

– longing for the perfect sexual relationship – generation. But she is, in some ways, an old-fashioned sort of person, and she made of friendship something very unique. We could be looking at this chart in terms of psychological development, and we would be tracking it in a very different way. I am looking at it the way she looked at it, and the way she was dealing with being who she found herself to be. We are watching her process of self-reflection rather than our reflections on her process.

She was now a trainer and she was also running the office, but now her **progressed Moon** arrived at the **opposition**. The first opposition signalled her first real rebellion against her mother and her decision to have nothing to do with authority. This time she had become an authority herself. However, she discovered, just before the progressed Moon opposed its natal place, that things were happening in the organisation that she did not like. She could not accept these things and she could not change them, so she left. She had achieved the recognition she had sought, and now she became aware of needs that could not be fulfilled in the world of her organisation. She rebelled, and left, seeking emotional nourishment from new worlds. She returned to nursing and worked in the labour ward. The progressed Moon was in Scorpio. She was in the labour ward but also operating as a midwife, delivering babies for her friends and others who sought her services. Good Moon in Scorpio stuff.

One of her close friends died of cancer just after her progressed Moon opposed its own place and conjoined Saturn. During this time she went into psychotherapy. Her mother had become very helpless – her father had died – and although her mother was in a nursing home, she had accepted emotional responsibility for her. She sometimes still struggled with her anger and resistance to her mother, but she also began to love her, as an adult loves, with responsibility and will.

As her Moon went into Sagittarius she began to break the friendship with the woman who had been her closest companion for the previous ten years or so. She has still had no relationships with men. She told me that she decided to see if a sexual relationship with a woman might be the nourishment she was lacking. She said, "I tried it out. I was open to it, but it didn't work. So I had to give it up."

Between the time of the lunar opposition and the next square, the incoming square to its own place, she got to know herself quite deeply. She was lonely much of the time, but she rediscovered her love of adventure – progressed Moon in Sagittarius – as one of her resources – in the 1st and then the 2nd house. She tried out all sorts of things, and developed herself as a teacher of various methods of self-awareness. She counselled people with weight problems and ran groups for people with various fears and inhibitions. She began to make new friends and went on hiking trips with people. She learned new inner and outer skills.

When the progressed Moon went into Capricorn, in the 3rd house, she bought a house in a new neighbourhood. She had never owned a house before and she found it in a neighbourhood she had not known – 3rd house response. By the end of 1993, when **Saturn** was in Aquarius in the 4th house, and **opposing its own place** – and having squared natal Moon-Mercury – she was established in her home and she had taken up something called "The Transformation Game." She was training to become someone who runs the game for other people. It is a game, played on a board, but set out in such a way that the insights arising from it can be psychologically and spiritually transforming.

When she came to visit me here in London, in July of this year, her progressed Moon had just gone into Aquarius, conjoining Jupiter in the 4th house. The lunar square is still two years away. She said, "The last time I arrived at the square was so lonely. It is only recently that I have really learned, deep inside, that I have always asked others to fill my emotional needs. To some extent that is just the way I am, with Moon in the 7th. But I have learned to live with loneliness too, and sometimes that fills an emotional need; loneliness becomes solitude. I always thought other people cut me off – and now I know it is often I who cut off. I need to be cut off from the flow between myself and another person, to find myself and the flow between my-self and life."

When I saw her this time, I could feel the transformation she had gone through. I had seen her transform herself before – Scorpio rising and Sun square Pluto – and each time it was deeper. She still wasn't in a sexual relationship, and she said, "I haven't managed to undo that one, and maybe I never will, but I don't feel cut off from life because of it now." She said, "This Sun square Pluto and Moon square Saturn is mine now."

I showed you this particular person's experiences with the lunar and Saturn cycles because I like the way she works with her life and I like the way she uses astrology. The thing about astrology is that it is a very simple, very elegant system. It becomes difficult when we try to put all the layers together and then interpret it for ourselves and our clients and friends! Lindsay Radermacher gave a talk about this at the last Astrological Association Conference. She asked, "How do you turn vast cosmic symbols into signposts and into road signs?" You have the richness of the imagery, and you have to bring it down to something that offers practical direction.

We have all experienced this as astrologers. You look at a chart and see an aspect. You think, "What does this mean?" As soon as you put a meaning on it, you come out of the realm of symbols that go back to the beginning of the birth of consciousness, and bring it down to, "Well it means this and that and thus and so." The difficulty is not only in translating it for another person, it is in translating it for yourself.

We find ways of expressing the conditions that certain aspects may represent. We articulate it, whether it be an inner or outer con-dition. Later, we forget that we were simply giving words, at that time, to something reflected by a particular aspect. We now think the aspect has a meaning of its own and we apply it whenever we see that aspect. We become trapped in our own definitions – slaves of our own concretising minds.

For the last few hours we have talked about the progressed Moon in a particular way. I have tried to evoke something about it, but have inevitably slipped into defining it. I hope you haven't gotten caught by the definitions, but I hope you have developed a taste for exploring the interweave between the Moon and Saturn. Just keep your eye on your own progressed Moon as it goes through the signs and houses, and note when it forms angles to its own natal place. Watch how this cycle interacts with the Saturn cycle. They represent together the ever-repeating, always the same and infinitely different experiences that we have as souls incarnated in this time-bound space, surrounded by eternity. Attending them faithfully allows a wisdom to unfold that nourishes us down to the roots of our common humanity. They are the warp and the weft of life, as revealed by the astrological chart.

We'll stop now. Thanks for an interesting day.

BIBLIOGRAPHY

Elliot, Rose, *Life Cycles*, Macmillan, London, 1993.

Greene, Liz, *Saturn*, Samuel Weiser, New York, 1976.

Rudhyar, Dane, *The Lunation Cycle*, Shambhala Publications, San Francisco, 1971.

Hillman, James, *The Dream and the Underworld*, Harper & Row, New York, 1979.

Hillman, James, *Re-Visioning Psychology*, Harper & Row, New York, 1975.

Odent, Michael, *Water and Sexuality*, Arkana, London, 1990.

Zohar, Danah, *The Quantum Self*, Bloomsbury, London, 1990.

ABOUT THE AUTHOR

Darby Costello studied psychology, philosophy and theology at university in America in the mid 1960s. After some travel, she returned to the USA to study astrology in Boston, first with Francis Sarkoian and Louis Acker and then with Isabel Hickey. In 1971 she went to South Africa for a brief visit and stayed twelve years. During that time she worked with the Museum of Man and Science, in Johannesburg, recording the art and practices of the samgomas, the diviner/healers of Southern Africa. At the same time she began doing charts for people, gradually developing a wide clientele over the years. In 1983 she came to London. In the first few years she developed her practice and began giving workshops and seminars to various groups, while deepening her own knowledge of astrology's cultural history. In 1988 she joined the Centre for Psychological Astrology, where she taught and supervised students.

Darby he wrote her first book, *Astrology,* for Dorling Kindersley's "Pocket" series, with Lindsay Radermacher. She then wrote three books of seminar collections for the CPA Press: *The Astrological Moon, Water and Fire,* and *Earth and Air.* She was one of four contributors to *The Mars Quartet,* published by the CPA Press in 2001.

Darby teaches and lectures throughout Europe and in other parts of the world. She is a teacher for the webinar schools MISPA and Astrology University, and is a visiting tutor for The London School of Astrology and the Faculty of Astrological Studies. In 2013 she received the Charles Harvey Award for Exceptional Service to Astrology.

Made in the USA
Columbia, SC
26 September 2020

21637275R00139